MY BEST YEAR EVER!

12 LESSONS TO HELP YOU MAKE THIS A YEAR TO REMEMBER

By Rachel L. Proctor

RaySquared Publishing Co.
Dallas

My Best Year Ever: 12 Lessons to Help You Make This a Year to Remember!

Copyright © 2016 by Rachel L. Proctor

The material in this publication is provided for information purposes only. Procedures, laws and regulations are constantly changing and the examples are intended to be general guidelines only. This book is sold with the understanding that no one involved in this publication is attempting herein to render professional advice.

Unless otherwise indicated, all Scripture quotations are taken from the Holy Bible, New Living Translation, copyright © 1996, 2004, 2007 by Tyndale House Foundation. Used by permission of Tyndale House Publishers, Inc., Carol Stream, Illinois 60188. All rights reserved.

Cover Design: LSD Design
Interior Design: Rachel L. Proctor

ISBN 978-0692660997

Printed in United States of America

Dedication

This book is dedicated to my late father, Cecil Ray Proctor.

"Always faithful"

TABLE OF CONTENTS

PREFACE

Years before I ever wrote a single sentence of this book, God told me I would be an author. I had no idea what my book would be about and much to my surprise the years that followed that prompting were some of the most tumultuous times I've ever faced. Looking back on it now I see that it was those years that shaped me into the woman I needed to be in order to write the words that I will share with you on the pages to follow.

A pivotal and defining moment in my life came when I lost my dad. Experiencing his untimely death changed my entire perception on life. It made me realize that life is very fragile. I was reminded of my own mortality. But it also ignited something within my soul that even to this day is unexplainable for me. It reminded me that tomorrow is not promised to any of us. Whatever you know without a doubt you are called to do while you are here on earth – do it now!

As I found myself putting the finishing touches on this book, I felt a sense of purpose wash over me as I changed my bio to reflect my new found status as not just a writer but as a published author. I say that because there were many days I thought this book would never happen. I can't begin to tell you how many times I thought about just scrapping the book idea all together. *It felt too hard.*

Starting and stopping during the writing process proved to be a blessing in disguise though because it made me think long and hard about Gods timing for my life. I learned that it was my job to recognize Gods timing, *not try to change it.* It reminded me that the things I went through really did work out for my good. Those events pushed me to finally birth my authentic story.

This book is my gift to you. God restored me by sending people to me who needed to hear my past so that it wouldn't become their future. I learned that anything really is possible if you believe. I learned that the words we speak do in fact shape our reality. I want to empower you with the lessons in this book so you can empower the next woman and create a chain effect that can be felt in your home, your community and all over the world!

I'm proof that you can live out your dreams despite hardships and unexpected tragedy. But you must be intentional with your life above all else. You must change your way of thinking because your behavior follows your thoughts. You must plan your day and not leave it up to chance. You have to give a considerable amount of thought to what outcomes you want to see and recommit yourself to them every day.

I know what it means to feel unqualified by your past. But it's my goal to use this book as a vehicle to encourage you to dream again. It's my hope and prayer that 'My Best Year Ever' will help you reflect on your past, discover the possibilities for your future and walk boldly into everything God has had planned for you since your birth. The lessons I've included in this book are ones that are very meaningful to me. They've helped me believe deeply in my own abilities and they are what fuel my desire to help other people believe in their unique abilities too.

Personal and spiritual development are more than just one-time incidents. They are ongoing processes. As you read this book and write from your heart on the pages provided, my hope is that you will open yourself up to an entirely different way of looking at your life and your purpose. I want you to recognize what you have inside of you. I want you to imagine the possibilities for this year and every year after!

WARNING: When you start to think and act differently, you will be stretched. You'll be uncomfortable at times. It takes time to break down mental barriers that have had their place in your mind for years and possibly

13

even decades. But there can be no growth without some growing pains. Here's to your best year ever!

x - Rachel

HOW TO USE THIS BOOK

My impetus for writing this book came from the overwhelming number of requests for prayer and mentorship from women I encounter on a daily basis whether it's through my role in public service, ministry or social media. Some days I am inundated with requests for prayer, coaching, mentoring and encouragement in general and I literally cannot respond to them all. I know that this book will be able to go places I may never have the chance to go so I want to use my *Inspirational Goal Setting Journal* as a way to "multiply myself". This way I can serve as the personal motivational coach to as many women as this book will reach!

'My Best Year Ever' is different from most personal development books you'll read. This book is a combination of my most powerful teachings, both Biblical and natural, and it's also a journal so you can catalog your own thoughts. I've included coaching questions within each lesson as well as journaling prompts in the back of the book to help you get the most out of what you will read.

WHAT IS LIFE COACHING?

Life Coaching as a profession is relatively new. Since life coaching is very different from other disciplines like counseling and mentoring, I thought it'd be helpful to give you some insight on what life coaching is and how I will use the tenets of it to guide you through this book.

As your coach it's my job to help you solve problems, reach the goals you set, create action plans around those goals and help you take the necessary steps to implement them. I also help walk you through decision-making processes in areas of your life where you may be stuck.

For that reason, this book is not designed for you to read it cover to cover in one sitting. I suggest you take no more than a chapter a day or even a chapter over the course of several days, and spend time working through the contents of what you read. That might seem like a lot, but having your best year ever does not happen by default. Exceeding your goals doesn't happen by chance. This investment of your time will have a big payoff if you apply the principles I'll be teaching in this book. Remember, above average achievements only happen by putting in an above average amount of work. Implementation of what you discover is where you will see transformation take place. Knowledge is not power. *Applied* knowledge is power.

Throughout each chapter I've included powerful reflection questions designed to help you dig your heels into the principles of each lesson to show you how they apply to you and where you are in life. The questions in the book are the same types of questions I would ask you if we were face to face in a real life coaching session. Throughout each chapter you will be challenged to reflect and take action on what you discovered. I also recommend that you keep your Bible nearby as you are reading. Many of the questions will require you to search the scriptures for revelation.

Each lesson is designed to introduce ideas and concepts that will spark a paradigm shift in your way of thinking. My goal is not to help you merely change. If you simply change you can change back to the former you and sink back into your old ways. My goal is to help facilitate a total transformation in your life!

"This means that anyone who belongs to Christ has become a new person. The old life is gone; a new life has begun!" - 2 Corinthians 5:17

Some of the questions that I'll ask you won't be easy. They are designed to really make you think hard about where you are now and where you envision yourself going in the future. The questions will cause you to examine your thought patterns and take note of how you view the world and your place in it. Again, I know that seems like a lot, but it's necessary to look at things you may not have considered before to get you started with identifying the barriers that could be blocking you from the peace and prosperity that is rightfully yours.

I also recommend you write down the thoughts and discoveries that come up for you as you read the book instead of waiting until later. Writing down those thoughts as soon as possible is important because you don't want to forget them.

You may be asking yourself *"How will I know if I'm on the right track?"* Well here's the fascinating thing about personal development that many people don't realize:

The answers are already inside of you.

I didn't write this book to tell you what to do. I wrote this book and formulated the questions to help you release any doubt and fear you have and do what you already know is right deep down in your heart. Here's a scripture that backs up this point:

"Knowing what is right is like deep water in the heart; a wise person draws from the well within."

- Proverbs 20:5 (MSG)

My only job as a coach is to help you pull out what is already in you. If you are open and honest with yourself and implement what I share in this book, it will only enhance and accelerate what God is already doing in your life. I don't think you would be reading this book if you didn't already feel a tugging on the inside of you telling you that there is something greater in store for you. I want to help you see past just having a *good* life. I want to help you create your *best* life!

HOW TO USE THE JOURNAL IN THIS BOOK

Journaling will help you figure out who you are, what you need and what you want but you only discover these things about yourself after you have written them down. It wasn't until I took time to go back and look at many of my old journal entries, some of them even decades old, that I saw how far I'd come. To go back and read my progress was amazing! To see how I'd matured spiritually in so many areas helped me understand better why I had to go through certain things to become the woman I am today.

As you are writing, keep your focus on writing your journal entries for *yourself* rather than for an audience. Never forget that this process is for you. This will take the pressure off as far as feeling like your journal entry has to be perfect or correct. Just write without editing and let your thoughts flow. More times than not, your immediate thoughts will be the most genuine ones so just write them down and don't over think it.

Always pray before you start writing. Ask God to make you receptive and sensitive to whatever He is trying to say to you in that moment and record the significant insights that God reveals to you in your time of prayer in your journal. Writing things down and reflecting back on them later leads to deeper understanding and wisdom around your trials and even your triumphs. Make sure you date your entries as well as include the time of day that you wrote it so that you can go back and easily reference what time period it was in your life.

I'm excited for you because everything you need to experience transformation is closer than you think. Once you get the courage to grasp what's already in your reach - you will move mountains!

Let's get started!

LESSON #1 – PUT GOD IN FIRST PLACE

"When we put God first, all other things fall into their proper place or drop out of our lives. Our love of the Lord will govern the claims for our affection, the demands on our time, the interests we pursue, and the order of our priorities."

— *Ezra Taft Benson*

How would you feel if someone who says they love you only gave you their time when they could manage it? I know what it feels like to not be someone's priority especially when it's someone I've given my time and resources to help. This is exactly how God feels when we don't make Him a priority in our life. Well I take that back - not just "a" priority but "the" priority in our life.

So, if you're spending more time in fellowship with another person than you find yourself spending with God on a daily basis, your spiritual and emotional life is out of balance and you will soon start to feel the pain of the void God should be filling. God will not bless anything that He is not the head of. We can't give God *our* plan and ask Him to bless it. We must ask Him for His blessed plan from the beginning if we want to succeed.

It's relatively easy to tell what your daily priorities are. What activity(s) take(s) up the most time in your day other than your job? Is it extracurricular activities with your kids? Is it duties at your church? Is it a relationship with a spouse or a significant other?

- *What are the first activities and thoughts of your day? Be honest. This may even require you to put some serious thought into this. Quite often the things that we do unconsciously like our morning routine are not easy to recall off hand. Think about it and list them here. (Point of Clarity: You don't have to include things like brushing your teeth and washing your face. I'm looking for things like having devotion vs. checking your social media and email accounts.)*

_____

_____

_____

_____

- *After you have created your list ask yourself "How do each of these activities bring me closer to God and to fulfilling my purpose in life?"*

_____

_____

_____

- *Next, ask yourself "Of the activities I listed, which ones are not enhancing my relationship with God?"*

_____

_____

_____

SET THE FOUNDATION WITH PRAYER

"Never stop praying." - *1 Thessalonians 5:17*

About a decade ago, I was appointed as the project manager for a building project we were doing at my family's early childhood education center. I was new to this role and it was interesting to learn all of the ins and outs of commercial construction. I was able to follow the project from start to finish. What was most interesting to me though was the fact that so much emphasis was placed on getting the foundation of the building just right. When I looked at how the project budget was divided up, a major portion of the budget went towards laying the foundation before any money was ever put into the structure itself.

In order for this year to be solid you have to get your foundation right from the beginning. That means God has to be at the center of your life. Pray about every move you will make; even those small things you think you can figure out and handle. Take them to God and watch each choice you saturate in prayer lead to better outcomes this year. Better decisions start and end with prayer. When you ask for God's plan from the very beginning, you will avoid needless mistakes in the end.

WHEN PRAYING FEELS POINTLESS

"If we endure hardship, we will reign with Him. If we deny Him, He will deny us." - 2 Timothy 2:12

In a day where overall morale is low and skepticism is high, it may be hard for you to see the good that can come out of suffering. Have you ever had an experience where you felt like God was nowhere to be found at a time when you needed Him the most? Well, you're not alone. Abraham and Sarah endured years of sadness because of their desire for a child yet Sarah was barren (Genesis 21). Elijah suffered through the desert for 40 days and 40 nights with nothing to eat and then had to hide himself in a cave from evil people in authority who wanted him dead (1 Kings 19).

It's a natural assumption to feel like God loves you when things are going well. But when things begin to fall apart, it's easy to become discouraged and feel like He's turned His back on you.

Isaiah 45:15 says, "Truly, O God of Israel, our Savior, You work in mysterious ways." Why would a God who has promised in His word to be with us in the time of trouble, hide Himself from us when we are at a breaking point? Well the answer to that is quite simple. He does this so that He can *show* Himself to us! God hides in order to reveal Himself to us in our weakness and suffering. But it's always in the place that you least expect that He will show up.

- *Have you ever had a season in your life where you felt like God had turned His back on you? What did you learn about the character of God through that season?*

_____

_____

_____

_____

I want you to really lock into this next part if you have found yourself in the middle of a season in which it feels like praying about your situation is useless. Maybe you even find it hard to pray? I've felt that way before too and I can actually recall each emotion I felt at that time. I was in a period of my life were I was just beginning my spiritual growth journey in Christ. I was still gaining a true sense of who God was and who He wasn't. At that time, I'd just finished reading a book that talked about the character of God. I learned that God was *omniscient* or "all knowing". I figured since He was omniscient, He didn't need little old me to inform Him of the things that were happening in my life.

And while on the surface, that statement is true; the fundamental truth of the matter is that it's not that black and white. By thinking that way, I'd reduced God down to a basic being that couldn't be touched, felt or connected with.

"This High Priest of ours understands our weaknesses, for He faced all of the same testings we do, yet He did not sin."

– Hebrews 4:15

I had to realize that God wasn't caught off guard or taken by surprise concerning the issues of my life. He was not hearing about my problems for the first time when I decided to finally pray about them. He knows every detail about us and He cares about the smallest things that go on in each of our lives.

"And the very hairs on your head are all numbered. So don't be afraid; you are more valuable to God than a whole flock of sparrows." – Luke 12:7

So if that's the case, why do we pray about our issues and problems if God already knows about them? What's the point? We must take the following things into consideration:

- *We don't pray to God to INFORM Him.*
- *We don't pray to God to IMPRESS Him.*
- *We pray to God to INVITE Him.*

When we pray we invite God into our lives for fellowship with Him, to grow in His grace and to develop our dependency on Him. It's essential to our spiritual development if we will ever become mature Christians. Prayer extends us the opportunity and the privilege to work with God to manifest things in our life. If God did everything for us and we never put any skin in the game *(like praying, fasting and repentance),* eventually we would start to take His grace and our blessings for granted.

There have been so many times that I have prayed a prayer and nothing happened. I prayed again and still got nothing. In that moment discouragement reared its ugly head and told me *"Your prayers are not working. God doesn't hear you so what's the point?"*

Listen, if you're ever going to defeat discouragement you have to remind yourself of what's at stake. Make the fight personal! The implications and results of your obedience (or disobedience) extend far beyond just you. As a matter of fact, it's less about you than you realize. It's our job to be a light in this earth that will shine in the darkest of places. You must choose to believe what God says even when you can't feel Him or hear Him.

You have to keep praying even when it seems hardest to pray. Just because it seems like God isn't giving you an answer is not necessarily an indication that you aren't doing the will of God. Actually it could be quite the opposite!

Remember: The enemy only fights people who threaten to expose his plots! So keeping that in mind, I used that as fuel and persisted in prayer to God one more time. And that time around I asked God to search my heart to see if there were any hindrances that were blocking my answer. Many times there was. And although I was challenged to remove the things that were putting a wedge in my fellowship with God, I grew in my faith and my character was built up as a result of it. I learned how to persevere in prayer until I got an answer. My faith was increased. My patience was developed. I learned what it truly means to endure at all costs.

So the next time you find yourself asking, "What's the use in praying about {INSERT YOUR ISSUE HERE}", challenge yourself to go deeper!

- *If your prayers seem to be hindered, what could be getting in the way that you need to acknowledge and deal with?*

_____

_____

_____

_____

- *Write down 3 scriptures that remind you that God is with you even when you can't feel Him:*

_____

_____

_____

_____

- *Matthew 6:5-15 shows us the Model Prayer. Read this passage of scripture aloud and list 5 truths about prayer that you glean from it.*

_____

_____

_____

_____

If you're not regularly starting your day off by communing with God through prayer and meditation on His Word, I would be willing to bet that you are spiritually malnourished. You wouldn't go days or weeks without eating natural food so why would you go days or weeks at a time without reading your Bible or praying? It's next to impossible to know what Gods will is, His promises to you and what He thinks about you if you are not talking to Him on a daily basis.

Remember time is not an excuse. Even 10 minutes a day can make a difference when it's done consistently because the most important part of this is the condition of your heart. Humble your heart before you do anything. Chances are you won't "feel" anything and that's not the goal. The goal is to make God your number one priority through what you do and how you plan your day. Your actions are a higher level of communication than your words. Show God you are committed to Him. And even if you don't get all tingly inside, your consistent prayer will cause God to move in areas of your life in ways you never thought possible.

Find specific scriptures that speak to whatever you're dealing with and combine your prayer time with confession of those scriptures every day. Your faith will grow and so will your faithfulness. Spiritual growth and power over circumstances in your life is the reward of continually making God your top priority.

- *What are three things that Satan has tried to use in your life to make you question God's faithfulness to you?*

_____

_____

_____

_____

- *Read 2 Timothy 2:11-13. Write down the truths in this passage of scripture. Use them as weapons to combat doubt around the faithfulness of God.*

_____

_____

_____

_____

LESSON #2 – CONFRONT YOUR GIANTS

"You're trying to escape from your difficulties, and there never is any escape from difficulties, never. They have to be faced and fought."

— Enid Blyton

Several years ago, I was having some pretty serious problems with one of my wisdom teeth. It'd grown in sideways and ended up pushing on the tooth in front of it so much so until it damaged that tooth pretty badly. This one little wisdom tooth was causing me so many problems. It's amazing to think about it. How could something that small cause that much pain?

And what's worse is that I'm a totally scary cat when it comes to the dentist. I will admit that the only reason I eventually went to the dentist at all one day was because the pain had become unbearable. You see, one of my biggest fears around going to the dentist is being put under anesthesia. And after I finally talked myself into going in to see her, I went in and reluctantly sat down in her chair. In the back of my mind I hoped she would say there was something other than having the tooth removed that she could do to stop the pain.

Antibiotics?

Pain medication?

Nope. She said the tooth had to come out.

Fear swept over me as the words that I dreaded flowed freely from her mouth. I don't think I even let her finish her sentence before I got up from the chair and made my way out of her office – *quickly!* The thought of the anesthesia and everything it entailed made me leave her office and start preparing myself to continue to deal with the pain because I was not having that tooth removed if I could help it.

And while not having the tooth removed that day eased the worries in my head for a little while, it did nothing for the excruciating pain I still felt in my jaw. So for years after that day I dealt with it. There were long spans of time when the tooth didn't hurt at all and I was good. But then came even longer spans of time when the tooth would hurt so bad it made me wonder why I just didn't suck it up and let my dentist take the tooth out. I would apply ice packs and heat packs; I took ibuprofen and all sorts of stuff to help me cope with the pain. And although many of those things did lessen the pain, it did so only on a temporary basis. The only thing that would truly stop the pain once and for all would require me to face my fear around the anesthesia and have the tooth pulled which meant I would have to deal with the anesthesia.

Over the years since that initial day at the dentist's office, I'd taught myself a little trick. I trained myself to chew on the side of my mouth that was opposite of the painful tooth. This coping mechanism kept me from taking action on what I knew I needed to do.

But as long as I avoided the real issue I would have to keep dealing with the pain. And as long as you avoid making the changes you know you need to make, you will continue to deal with whatever source of pain you're facing well into the future. You will keep getting the same results if you don't take measures to stop allowing certain things to remain in your life.

- *How much further along could you be if you would eliminate an issue that has been a reoccurring source of pain in your life?*

_____

_____

_____

_____

Over time we all build up what are called "coping mechanisms". These coping mechanisms allow us to function with a *dysfunction*. For me it was chewing on the side of my mouth opposite the pain. This allowed me to remain detached from the problem and it kept me far enough away from it that it allowed me to still look normal on the outside even though I was battling with pain on the inside.

The goal of this chapter is to help you examine areas of pain in your life and look at how not dealing with these things has affected your destiny up to this point.

- *If you tolerate a dysfunction, you won't be motivated to change it. What issues have you developed coping mechanisms around that are allowing you to function with a dysfunction?*

_____

_____

_____

_____

In order to get over your problem you have to get close to it. This will be uncomfortable for you. But if you want to ultimately uproot the source of pain you are going to have to chew on the side that hurts. That's the only way you'll get the motivation you need to start making changes.

- *When you think about the sources of pain in your life, what fears come up for you when you think about removing them? Would you have to possibly lose a friend or separate from a family member? Would it cause a shift in your employment?*

_____

_____

_____

_____

MAKE PAIN WORK TO YOUR BENEFIT

As I said earlier in this chapter, pain is a signal that something deeper is wrong. When a sharp pain hits me my first response is generally to stop and try to figure out what caused the pain. More times than not, I would probably ignore some issues in my life and fail to seek help if it wasn't for the signals of pain that made me stop and take notice.

Introspection, which is periodically examining your own mental and emotional processes, can prove to be valuable for you. It can keep a small issue from compounding into something bigger. Many of the floods in our life start out as puddles. Addictions and destructive

37

habits almost always start off small. So take inventory of your emotions to keep small things from growing and taking over your life.

- *Pinpoint an area of pain you are avoiding. A financial situation? A soured relationship? An issue on your job? Allow yourself to get close to the problem. This may hurt you and cause you some discomfort but it is necessary. How might this issue get out of hand if you don't deal with it now?*

_____

_____

_____

_____

- *Evaluate how not dealing with this issue has hindered your progress up to this point. Next, look at how it will continue to hold you back from reaching your overall destiny if you continue in this pattern. Write your thoughts about that here.*

_____

_____

_____

_____

- *What is the first step you can take today to help you start dealing with this problem? It can be a small step. For example, instead of trying to have a full conversation with someone about a tough issue, simply let them know that you would like to talk with them and set a date to chat within the next week.*

_____

_____

_____

_____

"When Uriah's wife heard that her husband was dead, she mourned for him. When the period of mourning was over, David sent for her and brought her to the palace, and she became one of his wives. Then she gave birth to a son. But the Lord was displeased with what David had done."

– 2 Samuel 11:26-27

In this Bible story we see King David who was known in other passages of scripture as a man after Gods own heart. That thought vastly contradicts what is happening here in this story. As a matter of fact, this happens to be one of the most scandalous stories you'll ever read in the entire Bible! One day, King David stood on the roof of his palace and he was walking along the edge of the roof. While he was up there he caught a glimpse of a beautiful woman as she was bathing on the roof of her house below.

She captivated King David and for this reason he sent for her. Her name was Bathsheba. Once she arrived at his palace, one thing led to another and they slept together.

Now if this were a movie the storyline could have easily ended here. Many of the movies and television programming today paint us an untrue and sad picture which leads many people to believe that there are no consequences for their actions. We often get to see the fun side of sin without getting a glimpse of the ugly side which is the consequences we have to endure for our actions.

David and Bathsheba might have gotten away with what they did as far as what people could see until she came up pregnant! Once King David found out the news of her pregnancy, one bad move led to him making several other mistakes. When you read the entire text in 2 Samuel, chapters 11 and 12, you will find out that King David had an innocent man, which was Bathsheba's husband Uriah, killed to cover up what he'd done.

David arranged to have Uriah killed by having him strategically placed on the front line in battle. When the battle got the most intense the other men were ordered to withdraw from Uriah. After Uriah was killed, David thought he was in the clear. He thought his tracks were covered. Eventually God exposed what David had done and he had to face serious consequences. The major one was that the baby Bathsheba gave birth to ended up dying (2 Samuel 12:18).

Now, if you are familiar with David, when you think of his life, one of two events probably come to your mind. You either remember the time young David slew the giant Goliath; or you remember this story I just recapped where David committed adultery with Bathsheba. Both events were pivotal moments in the life of David. When David fought Goliath, he revealed his humility. In the second story when he committed sin with Bathsheba, he revealed his humanity. When David fought Goliath, he proved that he was a man of faith. When he gave in to sin, David proved that he was also a man of the flesh. When David met a giant named Goliath, we are privileged to witness his greatest victory. When David met Bathsheba, we are forced to watch his greatest defeat.

Up until this moment, David had never lost a battle. He was a man of war. Every time he stepped onto a field of combat, David won the battle and walked off the field a victor. However, when David entered the arena of combat within his own heart, he was defeated by a giant far more powerful than Goliath could have ever hoped to have been.

At the very root of David's problems, we find a King who was out of place and wasn't where he belonged. If David had been out on the battlefield with his soldiers instead of hanging around the palace it's possible that this incident with Bathsheba could have been avoided. Some Bible scholars have suggested the reason for him not going out to battle was that David may have been battling depression, or having a "mid-life crisis." In either event, he wasn't where he belonged and he became idle which is often the first step of a downhill slide.

It may be all too easy to draw the conclusion that Bathsheba should share in David's guilt as a willing participant, or if nothing else, you may feel she was an immodest woman who had no business bathing where someone could see her. But again we must take into account that in that society's governmental system, the King was the absolute authority. If Bathsheba was summoned to King David's palace, then she had to come or she would risk execution for defying the Kings orders. And most likely Bathsheba's bathing was not in a public place. More than likely she was behind the walls of an enclosed courtyard.

Seldom do we set out at first to commit sin. Had she been unmarried, he would have been within his rights in pursuing her as a wife. His inquiry would not have been improper in that case. But by the time he was told that she was married, David had already reached the point of no return and his lustful desires outweighed his good sense.

• *Have you ever been in a compromising situation in which you felt like you were at the point of no return? Read 1 Corinthians 10:13 and write down the solution that it suggests you follow if you find yourself in that place.*

_____

_____

_____

_____

If we really want to understand the nature of the giant that dwelled within David's heart, we need to look back at 2 Samuel 5:12-13. We are told there that God had blessed David and established his kingdom. We are also told that David recognized the hand of divine providence at work in his life. But, we are also given a piece of distressing news as well. Verse 13 says *"And David took more concubines and wives out of Jerusalem."*

So what's wrong with this? After all, David is a mighty King. He is undefeated on the field of battle. He has expanded the kingdom. He has built a great army and placed the right men in all the key positions. He has led the nation in growth militarily, financially, and spiritually.

But what David did in verse 13 was in direct contradiction to the word of God in Deuteronomy 17:14-17. There, the King was forbidden to do three things:

1. *He was not to accumulate horses.*
2. *He was not to accumulate wives.*
3. *He was not to accumulate gold and silver.*

Specifically the scripture reads in Deuteronomy 17:17, *"The king must not take many wives for himself, because they will turn his heart away from the Lord. And he must not accumulate large amounts of wealth in silver and gold for himself."*

David had honored God's command regarding items one and three. David had disabled the horses taken in battle (2 Sam. 8:4). He also dedicated the gold and silver taken as spoil in battle to the Lord (2 Sam. 8:7-12). But, he disregarded what God said about accumulating wives.

David had problems with a spiritual giant named "lust." You may not battle that one, but you know the name of the one you do battle with. In fact, if you have never done it, it might be good for you to identify your giant. Admitting that it exists is the first step in seeing it defeated.

- *Think about an area of temptation in your life that you find hard to resist. Could this be a giant in your life?*

_____

_____

_____

_____

When we take a deeper look at David's downfall, there are several factors that played a part in his giant gaining the power to attack his life. First, as a King, David should have led his men into battle instead of being at home while they were out fighting. He was neglecting his duties to a certain degree. Secondly, an idle mind creates a devils workshop. David was in bed when he should have been out in battle. Idleness gives your mind plenty of time to wander in areas where it shouldn't.

David also enjoyed absolute success and victory over all the enemies of Israel. Success can be a heady thing. You are never more vulnerable than when you have just enjoyed great success. People tend to develop a feeling of invincibility. David knew that God was with him. He may have let that knowledge go to his head.

- *If the scripture tells us there is a way out (1 Corinthians 10:13), why do you think it's so hard to not give in to temptation at times?*

_____

_____

_____

_____

When people are going through hard times, they become very dependent upon the Lord. There is no room for pride when you are depending on the Lord for everything you need. But when success comes and you have everything you want, it is easy to become lifted up in pride.

I am sure there are other things I could pinpoint about David here, but what you need to understand is that he could have prevented what happened had he taken the proper steps to safeguard his heart and mind. You see, David's giant, and the giants we face do not usually come from *without*. They come from *within*. Therefore, we must be certain that our spirit is fortified. This will allow us to do battle with the giants that lurk within our own hearts and gain the victory over them.

- *After reading this story about David, in your own words talk about how David's fall and redemption mirrors God's love for us.*

_____

_____

- *What is your response when you are confronted by a consequence of sin? Have you ever blamed someone else for causing it? Do you accept responsibility right away?*

- *How can having to deal with the consequences of sin instead of God taking away the consequences actually help you grow deeper in your faith? What would it show you about God and His nature?*

MY LONG DRIVE

From time to time, I go visit one of my sisters who lives about 2 hours away from me. It's a relatively easy drive since much of it is a long stretch of highway. I just put my car on cruise control, cut on my iPod and roll out.

47

After I have been driving for a while, if I'm not paying attention, I'll start to drift over onto the shoulder of the highway. The only thing that gets my attention is what they call "rumble strips". These rumble strips cause a loud vibrating noise in the car when your tires drive over them. The goal of a rumble strip is to serve as a preventive measure and reduce car accidents due to inattentive drivers on the road.

The warnings that the Holy Spirit gives us are like these rumble strips. Have you ever been in limbo with a situation or a decision in your life and you felt a tugging or a little small voice that told you:

"Don't do that."

"That won't end well if you go that route."

Even if you didn't hear a voice per se, it could be that you just felt uneasy about it. Those are spiritual rumble strips that come to warn us when we are veering too far off from Gods path for our life. They come to remind us of how we should live as believers. When we look at David's mistake, we can learn how to set up rumble strips in our lives and use them as a compass for right living.

I know I've talked a lot about David's mistake but there is an upside to all of this. The beauty of this story is that God is a God of grace. He would rather forgive us than judge us. After David gets called out by the Prophet Nathan (2 Samuel 12:1-7) his knees hit the floor in prayer and he comes clean with God and asks for forgiveness. And ultimately God did forgive him and continued to write an amazing story with David's life. God cares more about your next step than He does your misstep.

We should also remember that God will bestow His grace on us but that doesn't mean there won't be consequences in our life for the decisions we make. If I rob a bank and get caught I will go to jail. If I sincerely pray and ask God to forgive me for robbing that bank, He will absolutely forgive me. But I will still have to serve my time. God's forgiveness of our sins does not negate the consequences we may have to face.

- *In confessing sin to God, we don't escape the consequences, but God does forgive and forget our sin forever. However, we don't want to use the knowledge of that as an excuse to sin. How can you protect yourself from getting caught in the middle of tempting situations? List 3 scriptures that support your response.*

_____

_____

_____

_____

It's important to have the right people around you to hold you accountable and tell you the truth. Hearing the truth is not always easy but it will help you avoid doing things you can't reverse. Having the right person in your life will help you stay in your lane and away from the edge of compromise. They will help you to see ahead and point out negative consequences before you have to experience them. I don't believe God intended for us to learn everything by having to experience it for ourselves. He sends examples through His word as well as through people around us to teach us the lessons we need to learn to help us stay on track.

In the Psalms, David was quick to ask God to do an examination on his heart because he knew that he was prone to hidden sin and other unhealthy habits. This is why he was the apple of God's eye. He knew that if these things were left unchecked, they could creep in and take God's place in his heart. This is a Psalm that David wrote:

"Search me, O God, and know my heart; test me and know my anxious thoughts. Point out anything in me that offends You, and lead me along the path of everlasting life."

- Psalm 139:23-24

And while the easiest way to know if you are on the edge is to test it by Gods word, here are a few things I want you to consider as I close this chapter out. If you really let them soak in I feel confident they will help you experience victory over the *internal* giants you deal with. Answering these questions will help you set up some "rumble strips" to create spiritual boundaries in your life:

• *What are some places that you go to that cause you to be at your weakest moment spiritually? Maybe it's a place that evokes memories of a bad relationship or a destructive habit you once had? List them here.*

_____

_____

_____

_____

• *If you know you are tempted to do something that you wouldn't want anyone else to know about, think about how that situation would play out in the public if others were to find out. Could it ruin your witness for Christ? Write your thoughts here.*

_____

_____

_____

_____

• *What things upset you and really cause you to go off the emotional deep end? How does putting yourself in these*

situations cause you to be vulnerable and open to making
poor choices?

_____

_____

_____

_____

- *What things do you need to do physically to stop*
falling into sin?

_____

_____

_____

_____

Believe me, you won't always feel like letting God have full control. You won't always feel like working on a relationship or loving others and being kind but that's why you can't live by your emotions and what you feel. Emotions and feelings are fickle. They are temporary and can change in a moment's notice. That's why I try to avoid making major decisions when I'm tired, hungry, lonely or upset.

"The human heart is the most deceitful of all things, and
desperately wicked. Who really knows how bad it is?"

- Jeremiah 17:9

If you wait to feel like doing what you are supposed to do then chances are you will never do it. That's not even our nature as human beings anyway. We have to crucify the flesh because our natural instincts will always lead us to do what feels right to our flesh which may not always be the right thing to do in Gods eyes.

"So I say, let the Holy Spirit guide your lives. Then you won't be doing what your sinful nature craves. The sinful nature wants to do evil, which is just the opposite of what the Spirit wants. And the Spirit gives us desires that are the opposite of what the sinful nature desires. These two forces are constantly fighting each other, so you are not free to carry out your good intentions. But when you are directed by the Spirit, you are not under obligation to the law of Moses." - Galatians 5:16-18

- *David made a huge mistake in his life as we can see through reading about his story yet God called him the 'Apple of His Eye'. Why should you never think your sin is too bad to forgive?*

_____

_____

_____

_____

Temptation is an enticement to sin against the will of God for your life but remember that there is always a way out. We have free will so it's up to you to predetermine in your mind that you will not give in to sin. Pray and call on God when the temptation becomes the strongest. You can rely on the strength of God to carry you through those moments and help you experience victory over your giants.

LESSON #3 – MOVE FROM FEAR TO FAITH

"Faith is to believe what you do not see; the reward of this faith is to see what you believe."

- Saint Augustine

Most people I know have no shortage of great ideas. The problem comes in when it's time to implement the ideas. They have no idea where to start. They struggle with what the first step should be. Let's face it. An idea is only as good as its execution.

I see people full of potential everyday whether it's in my Facebook newsfeed or just around the way. But unfortunately far too many people never act on their inspiration. They talk about it but they never take action. But you have to learn to be ok with moving forward despite the unknowns and take the step anyway.

I want to start this chapter off by talking about your mindset. Your mindset is the beliefs, values, attitudes and thoughts that you carry within you. Your mindset is constantly being shaped by the things that happen to you and around you.

Not long ago, I was at a place in which I could never seem to get it together. I would have a great idea and I would be totally motivated in the beginning, but then for one reason or another, the big dream bubble popped! In other times, I could never find the courage to simply start a project.

But after a while it began to hurt too bad financially, emotionally, mentally, and spiritually to stay the same. When I reached the point where I would rather have felt the discomfort of change and growth more than the frustration and pain of remaining the same, I took action. I began to get clear signals from God that it was time to move and nurture the seed He planted in me years ago. When I made up my mind to let absolutely nothing stop me, I saw divine providence move with me. Little by little my fear was replaced with faith. That's why you are reading this book today. I had to change the way I thought. I had to question myself about what I was saying about my life and what I could have. Those are things I want you to consider. What are you saying about your life and what you can have?

- *What do you find most difficult about applying the faith you have been taught in church and in the Bible to your own life?*

_____

_____

_____

_____

"For therein is the righteousness of God revealed from faith to faith: as it is written, the just shall live by faith."

- Romans 1:17 (KJV)

Your dreams are possible because God is for you! It can feel uncomfortable and downright unnatural at times to do things differently and trek down an uncharted course. I know this feeling and I can relate. But if you are ever going to get different results, you've got to make stepping out of your comfort zone a way of life.

Your vision should be about a purpose that's bigger than you. If you can figure out how you are going to get it done then it's not big enough! For too long that voice in your head has told you that maybe your naysayers were right. It tells you that your dream is ridiculous. It urges you to just play it safe and stick to what you know. But in order to have your best year ever you have to gain the courage to silence that voice once and for all! That's exactly what I want to impart into you in this chapter.

- *What's keeping you from moving forward? It's critical that you own, confess and understand the root of the emotions that are keeping you stuck right now. The big question is "What fears do you have around finishing the task set before you?" Write your thoughts here.*

If you feel like you're not ready I'm here to tell you, more times than not you will have to start before you actually feel ready. And I'm stressing to you that the thing that has your stomach in knots right now is only a "feeling" and feelings change. Your feelings are not facts. You have everything you need inside of you to do what God is calling you to do. He will never send you into a battle that you're not equipped to fight. You won't always have all the details but that's where having faith comes in.

Maybe you have been spending all your time trying to live up to others expectations or even worse, maybe you have spent your life trying to live them down? Holding on to these types of false beliefs will keep you stuck in destructive patterns of behavior. Maybe you were repeatedly told as a young child that you would never achieve anything and now it's become so ingrained in your mind that you believe it? Well, you have the power to break those bonds off of your mind and change the course of your life!

STAND YOUR GROUND

Some years ago my pet Chihuahua, "Platinum" passed away. He'd gotten ill and we had to make the tough, heart breaking decision to lay him to rest. He was so special to me and if I could have had it any other way, he would still be here with me. He was not just any old Chihuahua either. He was what is called a "Teacup" Chihuahua. So he never got any bigger than 4-5lbs.

He was very protective of me as his owner too. And even though he was small, you couldn't afford to let the size fool you! He was super tiny but you could never convince him of that. He had what they call "Napoleon Syndrome" on steroids! I really believe deep down inside he thought he was a pit bull or something. He wasn't afraid of anything or anyone. I mean nothing could strike fear in his heart. He strutted around our neighborhood like he owned it. Anyone who thought they were going to cross him the wrong way had another thing coming. I could fill up this chapter with funny stories about my dog and his antics but I will spare you the additional details.

Most people that met my dog were afraid of him right off the bat. He could smell fear from a mile away. He could put even the toughest man on the run with a single bark. Many of my friends that came around him had a very real fear of my dog. The funny thing about that is they feared what they had control and dominion over. All you had to do was pick him up and slide him to the side to get him out of your way if you wanted to. He was so small that even if he did manage to bite you it wouldn't do much damage.

But he fed off of people's obvious fear of him. That's what fueled his ferociousness. The more you showed that you were afraid, the more he barked. But eventually, I finally had one friend who wised up. When they came over and my dog started the antics, they just sat still and ignored him. He continued to bark and growl and he even drew in closer to them to see if that could startle them but they didn't budge. After a few moments of that, my dog retreated to his pillow knowing full well he was defeated because what he tried to do didn't work on them. And it was all because my friend made the choice to just stand still. They didn't try to fight him back. They knew he really couldn't do anything so why bother. They had absolutely nothing to fear because they had the upper hand.

"My God sent His angel to shut the lions' mouths so that they would not hurt me, for I have been found innocent in His sight." – Daniel 6:22

This story is about when Daniel was thrown in the lion's den and it is a remarkable testament to the faithfulness of God when we put our complete trust in Him in moments of crisis. You should go back read the entire chapter to get the full layout of the story. When you read it you will see that he was able to go to sleep after being thrown in a pit of lions. Can you imagine having that type of peace in the middle of a life threatening situation? Daniel was undisturbed because He knew that God was stronger than the lions. He had a fence of protection around him. There was no need for him to get worked up about what he saw. It didn't matter because those things were powerless over him. Really what Daniel was doing was exercising his God given authority over what he saw. You and I have that same power today. Don't be moved by appearances. God is bigger than any circumstance you will face. So you don't have to fear anything (or any Chihuahua) that you will encounter.

"The Lord Himself will fight for you. Just stay calm."
– Exodus 14:14

Starve your fear and feed your faith. Be unmoved, unwavering and unshakeable! When you change how you look at things, the things you look at will suddenly change! Look at them through the eyes of faith.

- *Why do you think it's hard to let go of fear and trust God with your future? Think about a time when God made a way for you in the past. How can you use that time as a reminder of His faithfulness to you in the present?*

_____

_____

_____

_____

- *Was there a time when you were fearful and acted out on that fear instead of trusting God? What happened?*

_____

_____

_____

_____

TAKE ONE MORE STEP

In my line of work I often have meetings that cause me to have to be a part of frequent evening meetings. One night after a meeting, I had to make a quick run to the grocery store. I needed to grab a couple of essentials before the next day. I was tired so good thing for me there was a grocery store on my direct route home so I decided to stop there. I hopped out of my car and took quick paces toward the store entrance. As I got closer to the doors, I expected them to slide open and welcome me in as they always do. Well this time that didn't happen. I got closer and closer but the doors didn't open.

Was the store closed? Maybe they locked this particular door after a certain hour and I wasn't aware? Should I turn around and go down the breezeway to see if the other set of doors were open?

My eyes glanced at the store hours listed on the plate glass window. According to what was listed the store didn't close for another 4 hours. I could even see people walking around inside the bustling store despite the late hour. So why wouldn't these doors open as they always had?

Just as I was about to walk back to my car, almost as if guided by some external force, I took one more step forward and - voila! The doors slid open!

The store wasn't closed. The doors weren't locked. I just needed to take another step forward. You see what happened was the sensors that triggered the doors to open couldn't detect me in the current place I was in. I had to move closer into the proper area so the sensors could pick up my movement and then and only then would the doors open.

Have you ever gotten discouraged in the pursuit of your dreams? You know God told you to do something but absolutely no doors seem to be opening for you? If that describes you, before you decide to turn around I want to encourage you to take one more step!

I can remember countless times when I just wanted to be done. And if that meant taking the easy way out just to get some relief from the struggle then that's what I would do. I had become fed up with trying and failing. I couldn't fathom the thought of giving it another shot just to wind up disappointed in the end. Listen, I have experienced some of my greatest moments of discouragement just before God gave me a major breakthrough.

But even if we choose to abandon the mission and give up on ourselves - God doesn't give up on us! He has a plan and a purpose for our struggle. And just like that instinctive move at the grocery store, God can give you just enough strength to take that one critical step. That one step can be the tipping point between defeat and total victory.

- *God doesn't promise us a life of ease, but He does give us Biblical examples of His faithfulness. Search the scriptures and find 3 scriptures that you can use as encouragement to start trusting God with your next step. List them here.*

_____

_____

_____

_____

Now is not the time to turn around. Don't step backwards to look for an easier way out. Keep going forward. Even if you have to take a step afraid, know that God is with you. As long as your actions are in line with God and His will, He'll make the way and open the door. But you have got to move closer in faith.

It's the enemy's job to make God's way seem impossible. He wants to make you forfeit your divine blessing. He likes to present you with bogus options disguised as "opportunities" to distract you from the path that leads to your miracle. He wants to stop you before you get to your tipping point. But your true breakthrough lies in your faith to trust God and take the next step.

"Jesus looked at them intently and said, "Humanly speaking, it is impossible. But with God everything is possible." - Matthew 19:26

- *Philippians 1:6 says, "And I am certain that God, who began the good work within you, will continue His work until it is finally finished on the day when Christ Jesus returns." How does knowing this give you confidence in taking your next step?*

_____

_____

_____

_____

LESSON #4 – WAIT ON GOD'S TIMING

"God may withhold an answer to prayer until we relinquish control of the outcome and put our complete trust in Him."

— *Suzanne Elizabeth Anderson*

If there's one thing people hate to do, *it's waiting.* And why should we wait? We no longer have to pick up an encyclopedia and search for an answer. All we have to do is Google it. We have access to more information than we ever have had right in our pocket. We can order our favorite shoes online with the click of a button rather than standing in line at the mall. We can even book reservations ahead of time at our favorite restaurant rather than go in and wait for a table.

But even though we may find shortcuts to get some stuff we want, we can't rush God. In fact, in our walk with God much of it will be spent waiting on Him to respond. And while our natural inclination is to dislike waiting, this period of uncertainty can actually be a time of great personal growth if we keep the right perspective.

Several years ago I ran across a news story about a young man who was a former high school football star with a bright future. But his promising future came to a halt when he was wrongly accused of rape as a teenager by a young woman he went to school with. He was convicted of this rape and spent the next 5 years of his life in prison as a result of it. His accuser admitted to lying about the rape only after he'd done the time in prison. Ultimately he was exonerated a few years later. A bunch of questions came to mind after reading his story:

• *Why would God allow this young man who was in the prime of his life to spend 5 years in prison for a crime that we now know he didn't commit? This was time he would never get back.*

• *I wondered what was going through Brian's head as he sat there in his cell, knowing full well of his innocence, serving a sentence while his accuser lived in freedom.*

• *Why didn't God stop it? Why didn't He justify him before it was too late?*

Have you ever been at a place of waiting on God to answer? I'm not a gambling woman but I'm willing to bet that you have. Have you ever felt like you were at the end of your rope? Maybe you were in a situation in which you were about to lose your home and you did? Maybe you had a loved one who was facing a life threatening disease and instead of them being healed, *they died?* Or maybe you needed God to justify you like this young man in the story and instead of being justified you were convicted?

As Christians we're taught to always hope for the best. And generally speaking we should. But what do you do in those times that you have prayed so hard that your knees are numb? Have you ever cried yourself to sleep believing that when you wake up "this will be the day" but when that day arrives, you still got nothing?

Can you imagine in the Bible days how Martha and Mary must have felt as they waited for Jesus to come heal their brother Lazarus (See John 11)? I'm sure the sisters were pacing the floor wondering where Jesus was. And by the time Jesus arrived, Lazarus had been dead for four days already!

- *Describe a time when you prayed for something and it was not answered in the way you hoped for and in the timing you felt you needed it to be answered. What did you learn from that?*

_____

_____

- *What do you do when it seems like your prayer is not being answered? What helps you to keep praying through these times? List 3 scriptures to support your response.*

WAITING IN YOUR SINGLENESS

As I said earlier, I know waiting is difficult for everyone but I think it can really be hard for women who are in a season of singleness. If you have found yourself on a quest for the right mate, waiting on God can feel like torture. You pray and you plea bargain with God. You promise Him that you'll be forever grateful if He would just help you out this one time and send you the right person to marry.

I know for me, when I wasn't getting the clear direction from God that I thought I should be getting; it became very tempting to try and take things into my own hands. I convinced myself that God had given me a sign and I'd just missed it. But after several failed attempts at relationships on my part, God revealed to me that He was not going to give me somebody to share my life with until I became happy with the life He gave me to share.

I think some of that influence to take matters into our own hands comes from society's admiration of people who take charge and boldly make decisions. We reward initiative, not patience. We like people of action who dive in head first and grab the bull by the horns.

But the Bible is filled with people who waited for God to act, sometimes waiting for decades. Abraham and Sarah were both old and gray before Isaac was born (Genesis 21:2). Joseph had to wait for years before God reunited him with his family (Genesis 45).

There are times when God makes us wait because He is waiting on us to surrender our desires to Him. We have to trust that He will do the right thing by us because that's a part of His unchangeable character. Looking back on it, the right thing may not have always been what I wanted at the time but now I see where God was working on my behalf.

- *What is the most difficult part about waiting on God for the right mate in your opinion?*

_____

_____

_____

_____

- *Have you ever moved outside of God's timing?*
What was the result?

_____

_____

_____

_____

THE PROMISE AND THE ANSWER

Waiting on God requires us to spend a great deal of time in the gray area which is the space between the *promise* and the *answer*. The reality is we just don't know what's up ahead and it's the unknowns that can crush us. We doubt God because we don't know. We worry because we don't know. We falter and sometimes fail all because we don't know. If only we knew how the end was going to play out, everything would be ok. But we don't.

I can take a bad day. I can take a bad month. I can even take a bad year if I have to as long as I know how it will end up. For some of you it's a health crisis. For another, it's a question about your marriage or an uncertainty with a child that's in trouble. For someone else, it's restlessness in your soul. We all have areas of uncertainty where we are forced to hold on to what God has said because all of our other options have dried up. His promises are what we cling to while we wait for Him to work. He can't lie and He doesn't forget. He will deliver on time, every time. Who else can make promises like that?

I wish I could tell you that things always pans out perfectly according to what we feel is perfect, but I would be telling you a lie. You cannot make sense of what God is doing simply looking at things that are happening in your life alone. You must factor the reality of eternity into the equation. Eternity brings it all together. The promises of eternal life and the assurance of hope in heaven make God's promises exceedingly great and precious.

I'm not sure if I really have an explanation as to why God makes us wait or go through certain tragic situations in our lives. I'm not even sure we will ever find out in this lifetime. But what seems to be most important in anything that we go through is not our final destination, but who we become in the process. God wants to increase our faith and He wants us to know Him on a level that just going to church every Sunday can't bring you. Simply reading your Bible cannot get you to this place. Listening to worship music alone won't accomplish it either.

He wants to increase our faith and put us in a place in which we have no other choice but to trust Him. There are times when God will remove our options to show us how much we have neglected Him in our life. It's in those times when we have nothing or no one else, that we truly begin to learn who God is. Things may even get worse before they get better but James 1:2-4 instructs us to do the following:

"Dear brothers and sisters, when troubles of any kind come your way, consider it an opportunity for great joy. For you know that when your faith is tested, your endurance has a chance to grow. So let it grow, for when your endurance is fully developed, you will be perfect and complete, needing nothing."

It's through these times of great uncertainty that we learn to lean on Him the most. We may never know some of the answers to our questions in this lifetime. God uses our own unique journey to build our character and to help us connect with others in their time of suffering.

• *Sometimes short-term suffering can bring about long-term joy and peace. Have you ever felt like the pain you went through was worth it because of the end result? Describe that time here.*

74

LESSON #5 – BREAK THE CYCLE

"We are what we repeatedly do."

— *Aristotle*

"A woman in the crowd had suffered for twelve years with constant bleeding, and she could find no cure. Coming up behind Jesus, she touched the fringe of His robe. Immediately, the bleeding stopped. "Who touched me?" Jesus asked." - Luke 8:43-45

During the course of His ministry, Jesus performed many miracles. In the New Testament we typically see instances where Jesus lays His hands on the person in order to heal them or rid them of whatever it was they were dealing with. But in this case He never even touches the woman in the story. He was not looking for her. She came looking for Him.

The Bible says that she had *"an issue of blood"*. That meant she was hemorrhaging in her body. Her condition had literally ruined her life. In the Bible days under the law this woman was considered "unclean". Anything or anyone she touched was also considered unclean. As a result, she could not mingle with people in public or else she would cause them to be defiled too. She was basically an outcast.

She'd been plagued with this condition for 12 years. When you think about the average life span of people in that day, her condition had probably begun just after puberty. Therefore, for most or all of her adult life she had been in this sad shape. When you read her full story, we are told that she had tried every remedy she could come across. She spent all of her money trying to find a cure but now she was broke. Despite all of her efforts she continued to deteriorate inside. She was literally headed for death. Blood is life and her life was literally draining out of her body day by day.

But here's where the story starts to get a little better. This woman heard about Jesus somehow. She believed even if she could just touch His clothes her life could turn around.

She demonstrated great courage by approaching Jesus in that crowd. She was taking a big risk because if anybody recognized her she could be punished or even killed. A crowd like that might have gotten worked up and stoned her to death. But because she was so desperate for a change she believed it was worth the risk. She had run out of options and she felt down to her core that Jesus was her last hope.

When she was near enough to Him, she reached out a trembling hand and grabbed His garment. She held on to Him until she got what she came after! Then, *immediately*, she received what none of the doctors or their costly and painful remedies could give her. For the first time in 12 years she experienced healing.

- *Read Hebrews 11:1. What was so significant about what the women did? What was so unique about her faith?*

_____

_____

_____

_____

- *Hebrews 4:16 says, "So let us come boldly to the throne of our gracious God. There we will receive His mercy, and we will find grace to help us when we need it most." What fears or issues in your life keep you from approaching God with boldness? Are you ashamed of something from your past that makes you doubt your authority to approach God in this manner?*

_____

_____

I don't want to end the story here so let's go a little deeper. As I re-read this passage of scripture, I began to look at it differently. We never find out the woman's name but we do know her issue. She was plagued with a detrimental "cycle" that wouldn't end.

I don't think it was haphazard that God would show us in His word how a vicious cycle in our life can kill us if we don't take bold steps to break it. As a woman, her cycle was something that was a natural part of her. But in this case something that should have been normal had gotten out of hand. Something that should have helped her to be able to birth life into the world became something that would eventually end her life if it wasn't broken.

Simply put, a cycle is a periodic, repetitive sequence of events of a process that plays out over an indefinite amount of time. The period of time known as a year brings about the cycle of the seasons. You also have the life cycle which is birth, growth and then death. Moreover, you have what we call a *bi-cycle*. The wheels on it turn in a circular motion but in order for them to do that you must begin to press the pedals of the bicycle. This causes the wheels to turn and therefore it moves you in a certain direction. Many of the directions that our cycles take us in are not good directions. Just like this woman with the issue of blood, the cycle in her life was about to kill her if it didn't get broken.

Destructive cycles in our life typically start with bad habits that we form. Maybe you just did it once, then again, and then casually another time until now you feel like you have to do it or else something just doesn't feel right? Many of these things have a stronghold on us and they need to be broken. They can look like emotional habits, social habits, physical habits, spiritual habits or even financial habits. Habits are those things that are done often, and hence, done easily. They become automatic. We all have habits, whether good or bad.

Most of the time, you really don't realize that you are doing it but if you don't do it, you miss it. I read an article that stated about 50% or more of what we do is strictly done out of habit. I'm not talking about natural bodily functions that we do without having to tell ourselves. Things like breathing are not habits. Those are natural bodily processes that we will do as long as our body is functioning correctly.

I'm speaking of the things that we have done for so long that we do it automatically and without even thinking about it. Have you been entertaining certain cycles and bad habits that you need to break? It's time to confront whatever it is and get on the other side of it. You've been putting up with it long enough.

Believe it or not, it's these cycles that are keeping you from having your best year ever and from living the life God wants you to live. Detrimental cycles and bad habits are your enemy and you should treat them as such. You may think they are harmless but you will never overcome them until you treat them like the hindrance they are.

A big part of getting the courage to confront your cycles comes when you get tired of getting the same lackluster results over and over again. The woman in this story is unique because she receives her healing without asking for it. She simply touches Jesus in faith. He is surrounded by a crowd that is pressing in on Him from every side, but Jesus feels that one person's touch is different in a way that only He can perceive. This one woman is touching Him with great intention. She knows He has the power to heal her.

It's time to stop sitting by passively waiting on your breakthrough to come to you. There comes a time in your life when you have to get sick and tired of being sick and tired. Recognize when your options have run out. Get desperate and go after your healing, go after your peace and go after your breakthrough!

KEEP IT TO YOURSELF

There are times when it is better to keep things to yourself when you are truly seeking to make a change in your lifestyle. There are people that will try to keep you stuck because they have become content with less in their own life. If they get in the wind of you trying to make a change, they will try and convince you to stay stuck with them because misery loves company.

- *Can you identify a person in your life that doesn't encourage your positive growth? Do they encourage complacency instead? In what way(s) might they be a stumbling block to your progress? Write your thoughts here.*

_____

_____

_____

_____

"Don't let evil conquer you, but conquer evil by doing good." - Romans 12:21

83

Another way to look at this scripture in Romans is by looking at it as instruction to overcome bad habits with good habits. Here's how you can walk out Romans 12:21:

"We do this by keeping our eyes on Jesus, the champion who initiates and perfects our faith." - *Hebrews 12:2*

We've got to ask God to birth a new thing in our life through helping us form better habits. The scripture tells us to look away from the bad things that are distracting you and look to Jesus who is not just the author but also the finisher of your faith.

When we truly fix our eyes on Jesus, we may have 100 bad habits but it may only take us incorporating 5 or 6 good habits to override those 100. The more we focus on a bad habit or a weakness, the more of it we produce. It becomes bigger to us than anything else in our life because whatever you focus on is what will grow. It can even become bigger than God if we are not careful.

And if we are going to break bad habits and destroy destiny altering cycles in our life we have got to gain self-control and practice discipline. No discipline feels good while you are going through it. But discipline is your friend. It will help you become who God desires for you to be.

"No discipline is enjoyable while it is happening—it's

painful! But afterward there will be a peaceful harvest of

right living for those who are trained in this way."

- Hebrews 12:11

Nothing good happens accidently. You can catch a disease but you can't catch good health. You have to first see yourself in a different place and start adopting a new frame of mind. You have to proclaim out of your mouth that you have self-control through the power of the Holy Spirit. That is one of the fruits of the spirit that God desires for us to have.

"Well then, should we keep on sinning so that God can

show us more and more of His wonderful grace? Of course

not! Since we have died to sin, how can we continue to live

in it? Or have you forgotten that when we were joined with

Christ Jesus in baptism, we joined Him in His death? For

we died and were buried with Christ by baptism. And just

as Christ was raised from the dead by the glorious power

of the Father, now we also may live new lives."

- Romans 6:1-4

When something is dead it can't have a relationship with anything. So when you are dead to sin you should no longer have a relationship with it.

Like the woman in our story, you must get to a point in your life where you are tired of being on the merry go round. It's time to get off the ride. The first step to breaking a negative cycle is to realize that you're in one and that you're telling yourself a story about that cycle that reinforces it. You have to start telling yourself a new story that speaks to the power you have in Christ. The woman with the issue of blood took responsibility for her own healing by going after Jesus.

- *What situation(s) in your life mirror the issue in the life of this woman in our story? What destructive cycle in your life needs to end?*

_____

_____

_____

_____

- *What fear can you put aside in order for you to go after Jesus instead of waiting on Him to come to you?*

_____

_____

_____

_____

LESSON #6 – REST

*"You will never reach your destination if you stop and
throw stones at every dog that barks."*
— *Winston S. Churchill*

I'm sure everyone looks forward to rest at some point or another. Even with that, society places so much emphasis on productivity and work that it seems rest is hard to come by for most women. We go in to the office and work all day; we come home and microwave our dinner to save time, we scarf down our meal and then head off to our kid's game. We talk on our cell phones in the car and discuss more work stuff so we don't have to deal with it while we're at the kid's game. We come home and throw our dishes from dinner into the dishwasher so we are not stuck wasting time washing them by hand. But even with all of that, these so called time-saving strategies still have given us very little time to actually rest.

I would argue that as a society we are less rested than we ever have been even with all the apps, strategies and devices that are supposed to help us get more done in less time. It's not that we don't want rest, we just fail to find time to get it among all the things we say we have to do. But God has designed our bodies to need rest. And it seems that the more technology we have, the more crazy life becomes.

- *What "time-saving" strategies have you employed recently? Do you feel like they have helped you improve the quality of your life both naturally and spiritually? Why or why not?*

_____

_____

_____

_____

"As Jesus and the disciples continued on their way to Jerusalem, they came to a certain village where a woman named Martha welcomed Him into her home. Her sister, Mary, sat at the Lord's feet, listening to what He taught. But Martha was distracted by the big dinner she was preparing. She came to Jesus and said, "Lord, doesn't it seem unfair to you that my sister just sits here while I do all the work? Tell her to come and help me." But the Lord said to her, "My dear Martha, you are worried and upset over all these details! There is only one thing worth being concerned about. Mary has discovered it, and it will not be taken away from her." - Luke 10:38-42

This story begins when Jesus came to Bethany to visit the home of Martha, Mary, and Lazarus. They became close personal friends of Jesus during His earthly ministry. He had a profound love for their family, and it's clear from Luke's account in the Bible that Jesus made Himself at home when He was in their house.

Have you ever been like Martha? I mean where you feel like you have to always be "on" and "active" in some capacity, always doing more or else God won't be pleased with you? There have been times in my life that I felt useless if I wasn't constantly moving from one thing to the next. I wore busyness like a badge of honor!

"For we are God's masterpiece. He has created us anew in Christ Jesus, so we can do the good things He planned for us long ago." – Ephesians 2:10

Look at that. The scripture says that we don't create work to be done; we simply "walk" in what God has already preordained for us to do from the very beginning of time. If you can grasp that it can free you from the bondage of always feeling like you have to make something happen in your life. The scary part about this especially if you are a "busy bee" is that there will be times that making the choice to walk in what God has prepared for you may mean that you aren't doing anything at all. Here's what I mean by that.

Sometimes instead of actually doing a *physical* task, God may call you to pray or consecrate yourself so that He can download His strategy into your heart before you ever do anything. And I don't know about you but that's where the problem comes in for most people because prayer doesn't feel like you're doing anything. It can take months and even years for God to answer a prayer. So to keep praying day after day and still not see any progress can be daunting.

We have to be careful to resist the urge to feel like we can do *absolutely* anything. We can't point the promises of God at every pathway in our life. Philippians 4:13 tells us that we can do all things through Christ that gives us strength. On the surface that's true. We can do the things that God strengthens us to do. But that's just it. We have to make sure we are doing those things that He actually called us to do! There have been times when I have taken on projects I felt were good things to do but I wasn't effective in them. No one's life was impacted by what I was doing. That's because even though it was a good thing to do, it wasn't what I was called to do. God will give you strength to do the things He ordained you to do. So you have to make sure you are walking in what He has given you the gifts and talents to do.

- *Why do you feel the state of busyness is so attractive to women? What makes it difficult for you to slow down in your own life and "sit at the feet of Jesus" like Mary did?*

We read about Mary and Martha at the beginning of the chapter, and there we saw Mary sitting and listening to Jesus' words. Martha had an attitude because she felt like all the work was on her. After I studied this passage a bit more, some Bible scholars have even suggested that the two sisters were wealthy. This means it's possible that they had servants. So why was Martha so distracted with all this so called "work"?

When translated and broken down in its original language, the scripture says that Martha was worried. The word *worry* denotes an inward uneasiness. It also says she was troubled and disturbed. In saying this, Jesus cut straight through to the point. Mary wasn't lazy; she just had her priorities in line. Her relationship with Him was more important than all of the busy work Martha was doing.

Mary had learned how to prioritize. She discovered that rest is an inner quality and can be maintained in the midst of outer turmoil if certain principles are adhered to. It starts with making God your focus.

- *Worrying about our basic day to day needs is a big cause of unrest among many women. As Christians, our minds should not be preoccupied with acquiring the basic necessities of life. That's God's concern. He knows everything you need." Read Matthew 6:25-32. Write down the truths you uncover in that passage of scripture here.*

_____

_____

_____

_____

- *The work/eat/sleep/work/eat/sleep way of life was never God's intention for us. There's so much more to life than just going from one activity to the next. Have you ever found yourself in that pattern? What did you do to break that cycle?*

_____

_____

_____

_____

Planning and preparing for our future is essential but we should be careful that our minds are not preoccupied with what's going to happen that it turns into worry. We have to learn to leave the future in God's hands. There's a rest in God that you can never fully enter into if your mind is taken up with something that should be in God's hands.

"We can make our plans, but the Lord determines our steps." - Proverbs 16:9

Of course there are times when you should give some thought to what you'll do with your life. Pray about it and make sure your actions line up with Gods will. But once you've done that there's no use in constantly mulling over it. Worrying about what has to be done will keep you from experiencing the peace that comes with assurance that God is your ultimate provider.

WHEN EVIL PEOPLE PROSPER

"Be still in the presence of the Lord, and wait patiently for Him to act. Don't worry about evil people who prosper or fret about their wicked schemes. Stop being angry! Turn from your rage! Do not lose your temper— it only leads to harm. For the wicked will be destroyed, but those who trust

in the Lord will possess the land. Soon the wicked will disappear. Though you look for them, they will be gone."

- Psalm 37:7-10

It can become easy to get upset when you see people getting away with stuff they shouldn't get away with. The Hebrew word *fret* in this scripture means "to kindle with anger". It's an anger that brings about the kind of attitude that will cause you to question God and it can even provoke you to start praying prayers of vengeance. But I want you to remember God is not somewhere caught off guard by what's going on in the world. We can sleep like a baby because ultimately nobody gets away with any evil deed.

"But there is no peace for the wicked," says the Lord."

- Isaiah 48:22

We need to take a page from Mary's play book and sit with Jesus. Make this time a priority. I want to urge you to be diligent in spending time with God each day. Growing in the Word of God won't happen on its own. Study the Bible and apply what God reveals to you to your life. That's the key. The enemy doesn't mind you knowing the scripture. You only have true power when you apply the Word to your life. Just knowing it is not enough to fight this spiritual battle.

- *You can purchase "sleep" from the pharmacy but you can't purchase "rest". Find 3 scriptures that talk about the type of rest that God wants us to have and write them here.*

_____

_____

_____

_____

BEING DEFEATED BY DISTRACTIONS

We can also look at Martha again and see another issue that women deal with which is being distracted by things that are seemingly good endeavors. These types of distractions are harder to recognize because they are things that at first glance appear to be activities that would please God. Our service appears to flow from a gracious heart of genuine servitude. The fruit looks deceptively unselfish. But we must look at the root of the tree it's growing from in order to see the truth.

What distracts you on a daily basis? I'm sure you can think of some things that are obvious distractions like your phone, social media and email. But I want to take some time to deal with distractions that aren't so obvious

95

before I close this chapter out. These subtle yet deadly distractions are the ones that keep us going in circles and veering off from what God truly wants us to be doing with our time. Even our work in ministry can become a distraction if the position or the duties cause you to take your focus off the main thing which is building your relationship with God.

- *Consider the things that you could be achieving if you weren't distracted. Envision the best you. Write down what comes to mind.*

_____

_____

_____

_____

- *What does the best you look like physically?*

_____

_____

_____

_____

- *What does she achieve on a daily basis?*

_____

_____

_____

_____

- *How have her relationships improved as a result of becoming her best self?*

_____

_____

_____

_____

- *How does she serve others?*

_____

_____

_____

_____

- *How does she administer self-care each day? Note: It's important that you take some time out for yourself each day even if it's just 30 minutes.*

_____

_____

_____

_____

One of my own personal motivations that I had to get in check was that I was driven by affirmation and a deep desire to feel needed by others. Because of that, I would tend to say yes to everything that other people needed me to do in order to satisfy that need that I had. But on the other side of that, never saying no caused me to be constantly overwhelmed. I also stayed in regret mode, wishing I had said no to the endless requests and demands of others.

- *What does desire for approval look like to you? This can look like the desire to serve and do good things and receive compliments for your work in some cases.*

_____

_____

_____

_____

- *Martha felt confident that Jesus would take her side over Mary's. Why do you feel Jesus took Mary's side over Martha's?*

_____

_____

_____

_____

- *We can all be like Martha at times: Busy without a clear purpose and consumed with an endless to-do list. We can become too busy for other people or even too busy for God. Have you ever found yourself in Martha's shoes? Is prayer an important part of your daily life? Have you ever felt too busy to pray? What did you do about it?*

_____

_____

_____

_____

It can be easy to give God the leftovers of your day. But God must be first if our lives are going to work and be pleasing to Him. If you aren't seeing the hand of God over your endeavors, ask yourself what could be blocking it? Are you trying to make so many things happen that in all of your planning you have forgotten to consult with God?

- *John 15:5 says, "Yes, I am the vine; you are the branches. Those who remain in Me, and I in them, will produce much fruit. For apart from Me you can do nothing." Look at that last sentence in this passage. Are you giving God your plan and asking Him to bless it or are you asking Him for His plan first over everything else? In what ways can you make seeking God first a daily habit for you?*

_____

_____

_____

_____

LESSON #7 – CLAIM YOUR CALLING

"I believe there's a calling for all of us. I know that every human being has value and purpose. The real work of our lives is to become aware. And awakened. To answer the call."

— *Oprah Winfrey*

Some friends and I once took a road trip to Houston, Texas. It's about a 4 hour drive from my home. On the way there we had to pass through many rural areas to get to the metropolitan city. Most of these rural areas were far "off the grid" so to speak, so the GPS system we were using would lose its signal quite a bit. At one point during the trip, we began to get a little nervous because we were unable to get a signal for long time and we weren't sure if we were going in the right direction. Instead of panicking, one of my friends suggested that we pull over at the next gas station we saw to get directions and make sure we were on track.

A gas station soon came into view and we pulled over into the parking lot and went in. The building was small and run down and the building looked to be decades old. There was no one at the cash register and there were no other customers in the store so we began to look around for someone who could help us. There was an open door with a light on towards the back of the store. Hesitantly we went toward it and peeked into the room where we saw an older gentleman who looked to be about 70 year's old sitting at a desk reading a newspaper.

"Hello there!" he exclaimed.

We returned his greeting and began to tell him that we thought we might be lost and asked if he could help us. He then proceeded to tell us where to go.

"Just get back on the road and turn right after the railroad tracks. *You can't miss it,*" he said. "Then go past the Johnson's old farm where the grocery store used to be. *You can't miss it,*" he insisted.

He went on a little bit more and my friends and I allowed him to finish giving us what I'm sure he believed were adequate and detailed directions. We knew trying to get anything else out of him would be pointless so we thanked him for his time and left the store. My friends and I stared at each other in disbelief of what we'd just heard as we walked back to the car.

The man in the gas station *assumed* that we knew what the Johnson family's old farm looked like and that we had an idea of where the grocery store used to be. But what we soon found out as we got back on the road was that he forgot to tell us about the fork in the road and the new traffic light that had been put in further on up the road. And the problem is that while he may not have been able to miss it, *we did.*

Every now and then on this journey we may start off well. We set lofty goals and aspire to be something great. But as we keep on living, life can throw us some curve balls and unexpected events that eventually cause us to wander off the path we were on. Sometimes we go so far only to realize later that we were headed in the wrong direction. We move through life in good faith on the advice of others, thinking that *"we can't miss it"* only to find out later that there would be other unanticipated forks in the road that could throw us off.

Nothing is more heart breaking to me than observing a gifted person stumble through life without clear direction, focus, or purpose. In this chapter I want to inspire you to find your path and stake your claim in the world. I want to help you recognize and uncover the things you are deeply passionate about and find your voice. Maybe you're reading this and you are at a place where you've been trying to get a goal completed for the last few years of your life but comparison to other people has been a stumbling block for you? It's easy to look at people who have been on a certain path for 20 or 30 years of their life and it seems like you'll never get to their level. But comparing yourself to where someone else is, especially someone who has been in the game longer is the perfect way to give up on your dream. We don't give up because we don't have what it takes. We give up because we try and start at a place we should be finishing at.

- *Has there ever been a time when you felt as if your life lacked purpose? Describe how this felt. What made you feel this way?*

_____

_____

_____

_____

- *We have all had moments where we feel lost and without direction. When you feel lost or purposeless, what should you do? Who can you turn to for help?*

_____

_____

_____

_____

I'm a second generation entrepreneur. My late father started several businesses over his lifetime and he taught me a lot about hard work. He didn't even go to school past the 6th grade but he was still able to accomplish great things even though on paper he was looked at as unqualified. I often look at the struggles endured by people like my dad and others that came before me. They did so much more with so much less than we have today yet they achieved great things. Looking back at my dad's life and legacy taught me that there's never any room for excuses.

I started working in the family business when I was 14 years old and even though I had 1 or 2 hourly jobs during my teenage years, entrepreneurship is all I really know. As an entrepreneur you have the ability to create a unique platform to control your destiny and grow your impact and influence in the world. I know that not everyone who reads this book will feel called to entrepreneurship. And even if running a business is not your thing, you too have a unique opportunity to influence others through using that special "thing" that was placed inside of you at birth.

God doesn't make "spare" people. What that means is you're here for a reason. No one will ever have the unique talents, gifts or the perspective you have. And whether you admit it or not, there is something very special about you. You've been thinking it and feeling it but you just hadn't been able to put your finger on what it is. And when you walk in your purpose, it's that "thing" about you that inspires others to take action in their own lives.

I'm what I like to call *multi-passionate* when it comes to business. What this means is I love doing a lot of different things. I'm good at a bunch of stuff. Sometimes I wonder why God makes us good at so many different things. I say this because it can make it that much harder to figure out exactly what path you should take in life. Because I had the skills to do various things, it became harder for me to allow others to help me. I didn't want to relinquish control over the outcome.

At one point, that need for control caused me to attempt to learn how to do my own accounting and bookkeeping. I love to read and learn new skills. And although I'm very methodical in my approach to business, crunching numbers and keeping ledgers is just not my idea of a good time. That's why it's hard to believe I ever even attempted it. Now that's not to say I couldn't have learned enough about bookkeeping and accounting to do it myself. But taking on that task in my business wouldn't have been the highest and best use of my gifts or my time. I was *capable* of doing it but I wasn't *called* to do it.

I told a trusted mentor of mine at the time about how I was feeling overwhelmed because I was trying to do everything in my business. She told me something that has stuck with me to this day and I want to share it with you. She said I needed to *claim my calling*. I needed to stop trying to be good at a little bit of everything and learn to embrace mastery in the main thing I was put here on earth to do.

It took me a while to follow my mentor's advice and even now it hasn't been easy to strip down to just a few things to focus on because like I said earlier, I'm very passionate about many different things. And at that time I felt like I wasn't using everything God gave me if I didn't try to fit them all in. But it's actually quite the opposite. God desires us to do whatever we do in life with *excellence*.

"Work willingly at whatever you do, as though you were working for the Lord rather than for people."

– Colossians 3:23

Developing mastery is the only way you will see real success around your goals. Before I truly made a change in my ways, I remember working on a digital course for months one time and although I had an opinion about the topic the course was based on, God convicted me soon after I started about what I was doing. He told me that I was not truly called to speak on that topic. I realized again that if I wanted to have real success in what I was called to do, I had to keep the main thing - *the main thing*. I had to follow the real convictions of my heart. And when you start following the true convictions of your heart, you will come across as authentic and genuine to the people you are called to reach.

Once again, I was about to create something and champion a message that I was not called to deliver. I have to admit that it was even a bit cumbersome to try and create the course outline. After I sat with it for a few weeks I realized that just because I have a voice doesn't mean I should speak on it.

There were people who were truly called by God to speak on that same issue and I had to realize that I was not one of those people. At the end of the day, I learned a few new things from my research as I was preparing the course so all was not lost, but again I was *capable* but not *called*. I had to finally follow my mentor's advice and the voice of God and regain focus on what I was truly called to do.

- *Have you ever felt like you were missing out on something if you turned down an opportunity? Describe how you felt.*

All focus really means is to become singular in vision. When you know you're called to complete a mission you will have to deal with the opinions of others and their agendas. Everyone will have a suggestion on how you should do your thing. They will always find a way you could have done it better. But you can't afford to get distracted by what people are saying. Stay singular in your vision. When you get off track you tend to lose momentum. And when you lose momentum you lose power and confidence around what you are doing.

- *What makes focusing on just one endeavor difficult for you?*

_____

_____

_____

_____

Your calling should feel *natural* to you. Keep in mind that the thing that comes easy for you may very well be rocket science for someone else. Have you ever considered the possibility that you could hold the solution to someone's problem? Look at the things you have overcome in your life. It may even be something that once brought you shame.

- *What is that thing in your life that you overcame and achieved some level of success in? How can you use that to empower someone else? It's possible that this is the message you are supposed to share with the people who are assigned to you.*

_____

_____

_____

_____

"Do not neglect the spiritual gift you received through the prophecy spoken over you when the elders of the church laid their hands on you. Give your complete attention to these matters. Throw yourself into your tasks so that everyone will see your progress. Keep a close watch on how you live and on your teaching. Stay true to what is right for the sake of your own salvation and the salvation of those who hear you." - I Timothy 4:14-16

ARE YOU AN EXPERT?

Becoming an expert on a topic is not as hard as you might think. Simply put, in order to be an expert you must know more than the people that you're teaching. Now there are levels to this though. If you're a 5 on a scale of 1 to 10 then at least you know more than 1, 2, 3 and 4. So target those people and use what you know to help them get out of a bad place.

- *Did you get out of debt?*
- *Did you get out of a bad relationship?*
- *Did you lose weight and develop a healthy lifestyle?*

Whatever your experience in life has been use that to position yourself as an expert at some level. And even if you are able to tell people what not to do, that can be valuable to someone else's success and freedom from whatever situation they are trapped in.

Here's another piece of advice I want to give to you when it comes to claiming your calling: Don't tell everybody your dream. Not everyone will be able to understand what God told you to do and that's ok because it's not for them to understand. God gave the vision to you. There will be times when you don't even understand it but you have to trust that if God gave you the vision then you have what it takes inside of you to carry it out.

Unfortunately, there are many people who are jealous of other people's gifts as well. Let me encourage you to not waste your time on jealousy. Jealousy is a gift robber. Jealousy is an energy drainer. You should be so busy stirring up your own gift that you don't have time to be jealous of anyone else or even worried about people who are jealous of you.

When you start listening to people that don't truly support you or even those that just don't know *how* to support you, it can cause you to start shrinking so that they won't be intimidated or uncomfortable in your presence. Many people will project their own fears and past failures on you in the name of trying to protect you from being "disappointed" if things don't work out for you. But I want you to find your own voice and follow it. I'm convinced when you do this divine providence will follow you.

ALLOW YOUR GIFT TO PROFIT YOU

"Remember the Lord your God. He is the one who gives you power to be successful, in order to fulfill the covenant

He confirmed to your ancestors with an oath."

- Deuteronomy 8:18

Fears main goal is to stop you from reaching your destiny. If you do something well there's nothing wrong with being paid to do it. One of the best things in the world is to get paid to do something that you love so much that you would do it for free. If you use your gift in ways that honor God, *it will prosper you.*

Ask God to help you identify your gift. Don't let the enemy tell you that you don't have anything to contribute because everything God created has a purpose. Not only are your gifts the foundation of your purpose but when you put your gifts into action, countless needs among the people of God can be met through your obedience to walk in your purpose.

Here's how you can find your message:

- *What do people typically ask you for help in?*

_____

_____

_____

_____

- *If you had to teach something, what would you teach?*

_____

_____

- *What would you regret not fully doing, being or having in your life?*

_____

_____

_____

- *What were some challenges, difficulties and hardships you've overcome or are in the process of overcoming? How did you begin the process of overcoming it? List the steps here.*

_____

_____

_____

- *If you could get a message across to one group of people, who would those people be? What would your message be?*

_____

_____

_____

_____

LESSON #8 – DON'T BE LED BY EMOTIONS

"Your emotions are very unstable and should never be the foundation for direction in your life."

- Joyce Meyer

Our emotions are God given. In most cases, how you feel about something can be justified in some way or another. But before I learned this next lesson, I constantly found myself at one extreme or the other when it came to the level of my emotions. I was either completely going off the deep end or I was on the other side of that spectrum and found myself completely numb and withdrawn from a situation.

There are very few things I know of that are as volatile as our emotions. I mean, have you ever found yourself completely furious about a matter only to find out later once you got all the facts, that you completely blew it out of proportion?

Human feelings at their core are subject to change when our circumstances change. And falling prey to looking at your current situation or issues through emotional lenses is very dangerous. I say that because emotional reactions create a breeding ground for making permanent decisions for temporary situations. It's grievous to make choices based on how you feel in that moment because after some time passes it's possible that you may look at the situation differently. But the choice has already been made by that time so you are then left to deal with it. Sometimes you are left to deal with it for a lifetime.

"Now Adam had sexual relations with his wife, Eve, and she became pregnant. When she gave birth to Cain, she said, "With the Lord's help, I have produced a man!" Later she gave birth to his brother and named him Abel. When they grew up, Abel became a shepherd, while Cain cultivated the ground. When it was time for the harvest, Cain presented some of his crops as a gift to the Lord. Abel also brought a gift—the best portions of the firstborn lambs from his flock. The Lord accepted Abel and his gift, but He did not accept Cain and his gift. This made Cain very angry, and he looked dejected." - Genesis 4:1-5

Here in this text, we meet Cain and Abel, who are the very first siblings in the Bible. We don't learn much about Cain and Abel's personality just by reading the text at first but we do see Cain express a very strong emotion which happens to be *anger*. In the original translation of this text the word angry is stated as "wroth". The word wroth means "to burn or be kindled with anger or to heat one's self with vexation".

""Why are you so angry?" the Lord asked Cain. "Why do you look so dejected? You will be accepted if you do what is right. But if you refuse to do what is right, then watch out! Sin is crouching at the door, eager to control you. But you must subdue it and be its master."" - Genesis 4:6-7

This story takes an interesting turn because now God comes into the plot. He actually notices Cain and points out the fact that He sees he is angry. God cares more about us than I think we realize. I don't know if there are many other stories in the Bible that show Gods concern for us quite like this text does. The God of the universe stopped to check Cain on his attitude! And of course God knew what his problem was but I think this was Gods way of testing Cain to see if he would just come clean about how he was feeling.

Have you ever found yourself trying to hide your real emotions from God? He knows everything that's going on with us anyway. He sees when you have been treated unfair and when you have been betrayed. So why did God ask Cain that question? I believe this goes back to the fact that God desires to have a relationship with us.

117

If you're a parent, even if you don't know exactly what's wrong with your child, your instinct will tell you something is wrong even if your child tries to hide it. Your desire to connect with that child will lead you to ask questions. God not only wants to know us, He wants us to know Him as well. And that only happens through communication with Him.

God lets Cain know that if he would have just stayed calm and remained joyful that he still would have been accepted by Him. But if Cain didn't get his emotions in check, God warned him that sin was waiting for him.

"One day Cain suggested to his brother, "Let's go out into the fields." And while they were in the field, Cain attacked his brother, Abel, and killed him." - Genesis 4:8

We see that Cain chose to follow his own emotions instead of choosing to calm down and accept what God said as the truth. His emotions caused him to do something that was irreversible. He killed his brother. I'm not suggesting that you will ever get so angry that you will literally commit murder. But what I am saying is that you must take control of your emotions so that you do not commit murder with your mouth! We can say things that can be just as damaging as what Cain did.

- *Have you ever said something hurtful to someone you love that you couldn't take back? What did you learn about yourself from that experience?*

_____

_____

_____

_____

We learn several things about emotions when we look at this story of Cain and Abel. Cain did not control his emotions nor did he heed the warning he was given by God and as a result he:

1. *Killed his brother Abel.*
2. *Ignored Gods warning and disobeyed Him.*
3. *Ended up lying to God.*
4. *Missed his blessing and elevation from God.*
5. *Was cursed by God.*
6. *Obtained mercy from God.*

Acting on emotions is dangerous and can hold some serious implications if we don't keep them in check. You can take this to another level when you find yourself going to the extreme especially when it comes to emotions like lust, anger, jealousy, vengeance and fury. When you feel yourself getting to a boiling point, chances are you have now moved into the extreme zone! Extreme behavior does not always mean that you are behaving drastically or out of control. There are times when extreme behavior can look quite the opposite. Allowing yourself to be so upset that you withdraw and shutdown from everything also shows extreme behavior. It's just on the other end of the spectrum.

Whether you have reached a tipping point and you find yourself yelling and screaming uncontrollably or you have shut yourself off and went numb to everything going on around you, it's difficult at that point for any voice of reason to penetrate your heart.

One definition of extreme describes it as 'being farthest from the center'. God should be our center. He should be the anchor in our life that keeps us grounded. I used the word *should* because, no matter how hard we try, there will be times when we move away from this center. Extreme emotions are the antithesis of Gods character. When we move away from God and take the path Cain took:

1. *We end up doing things we regret later.*
2. *We do things that we can't undo.*
3. *We do things that cause us to overreact.*

I'm not bringing out these points because I want you to totally dismiss your feelings because the truth is we need our feelings. It's not wrong to have feelings. I just don't want you to let your feelings have you! They are helpful in many ways but you must keep the perspective that your feelings are not absolute. They should never be a basis for making decisions, especially decisions with long-term implications.

DON'T JUMP THE GUN

I'm sure if you think hard enough you can remember at least one time that you assumed incorrectly about someone or something all because you simply didn't take the time to get clarity on what was going on from the beginning? Going off of your emotions and making assumptions based on them can make you look silly in the end. We have to get out of the habit of immediately asking ourselves *"How do I feel about this?"* Some of the better questions to first ask yourself are the following:

1. What do I _know_ about this situation?
2. Do I _believe_ what I currently know?
3. Do I _accept_ what I currently know?

When you really take time to stop and ask yourself those questions, it keeps you from backing yourself into a corner in a situation you can't get out of.

Overspending, overeating, and plain old overdoing it are all emotionally driven activities. Shopping sprees and eating binges, even those that are celebratory, do very little for you once the fanfare is over. You're often just deeper in debt and a few pounds heavier once the smoke clears. Our heart is the seat of our emotions. That's why Solomon urges us in Proverbs 4:23 to *"Guard our hearts above all else, because it determines the course of our life."*

Staying high-strung about every little thing we encounter can bring on some serious health problems too. Stress and high emotions can lead you to believe that everything is a state of emergency. Stress is a catalyst for strokes, high blood pressure, cancer and other types of diseases. Staying under high amounts of stress and anxiety lower your body's ability to fight off disease and it's a leading cause of sleep deprivation.

I want you to refuse to stay stressed out behind stuff that *you don't know for sure*. Release the anxiety around "the thought" of something. Because really all you are doing at that point is managing the *what if's* of something but you're not dealing with the reality of it.

- *Was there ever a time in your life that you let your emotions get the best of you and you acted without thinking? How did that situation end for you?*

122

_____

_____

_____

_____

- *Have you ever found yourself imagining a scenario and conjuring up an event that hadn't happened yet? How did those types of thoughts prove to be unhelpful to your emotional, mental and spiritual health?*

_____

_____

_____

_____

When you are emotionally healthy, you are able to look at situations on a broader scale. It's impossible to see the whole picture when you're standing inside the frame. Have you ever noticed how easy it is for us to give good advice concerning other people's situations but when we find our self in a similar fix, we can't seem to figure it out?

This phenomenon happens because when we are looking at someone else's situation, we are separated from the emotions they are feeling because they are in the middle of it and we're not. And when you are in a situation especially an interpersonal relationship, chances are you have deep ties with the other party. The deep emotions you feel can cloud your rationale. That's why it's important that you only deal with what is factual in a situation so that you can see the big picture.

Here are a couple of reflection questions I want you to take some time to think about:

- *Go back and read Genesis 4:1-16. What did you learn about the character of God in His dealings with Cain?*

_____

_____

_____

_____

- *How did Cain's emotions contribute to his downward spiral? How can you use his example to help you set safe guards on your emotions to keep you from going down the path he took?*

_____

_____

_____

_____

LESSON #9 – LEARN WHEN TO LET GO

"Incredible change happens in your life when you decide to take control of what you do have power over instead of craving control over what you don't."

— *Steve Maraboli*

Many experts say that where you are in life right now is derived from the sum total of the 5 people you spend the most time with. Taking a serious inventory of who you're attached to will be one of the single most important things you can focus on in terms of paving the way to your best year ever. The wrong attachments can be destructive and even deadly. I can remember times in my life that I got off track. And after taking a look back on those times I could almost always trace the point in which I got off course back to a bad relationship, friendship or connection that I chose to open myself up to.

That's why it's imperative that you choose to connect with people that empower you and disconnect from people that drain you. Here's how you can tell the difference in your connections:

For starters, when someone empowers you they motivate you to be your own person. They don't try to manipulate you into who they would like to see you become. They're ok with you being the best version of who God created you to be.

At this point in my life, I know right off the bat when I'm dealing with a person who has a gift to empower others. Their speech is different. Their whole demeanor is different. Their natural tendency is to look at the upside of a matter. Their point of view, especially when it comes to obstacles or hard times in life is the complete opposite of a person with a draining personality. When I've encountered a negative person, I literally walk away feeling like life has been sucked out of me. I consider myself to be a pretty positive person most of the time but when I've had a run in with a negative person, afterwards I find myself having to retrain my own thoughts and speech back to thoughts that are affirming and uplifting.

The truth of the matter is that the people we fellowship with have a lot of influence on how we think and act. Relationships should bring out the best in you and help you raise the bar in your life. If they are not doing that then it may be time to disconnect. The great part about this is in most cases you do have a choice in who you connect with. I say in most cases because there are connections you will have that you don't have control over. I'll deal with that in more detail later in this chapter.

The courage you need to speak up and make changes is available if you really want it. This courage can only come from God. And when you really want to be free from the wrong thing, you have to fix your sights on pleasing God, not people. There will come a time when you have to make peace with the fact that it will be impossible to do both.

Whatever you're connected to will pull you in one direction or another. If you are attached to something or someone that's going in a downward spiral, if you don't choose to let that thing go, you will eventually go down with it because it's pulling you in that direction. And the reverse of that is also true. If you're connected with someone who is going up, chances are you will go up too if you remain connected.

"Do not be misled: 'Bad company corrupts good character.'" - 1 Corinthians 15:33

JUST BECAUSE BLESSINGS

"And the Lord said, "I will wipe this human race I have created from the face of the earth. Yes, and I will destroy every living thing—all the people, the large animals, the small animals that scurry along the ground, and even the birds of the sky. I am sorry I ever made them." But Noah found favor with the Lord." – Genesis 6:7-8

In Genesis chapter 6, God looked down from heaven and saw a problem with His creation. It wasn't with the animals or the plant life that He had a problem with. It was with the humans He'd made. Sin was spreading throughout the land. It was taking over and beginning to control the way people thought and acted. As a result God chose to destroy much of what He had created and start over again using a man named Noah and his family as that new beginning. Noah walked faithfully with the Lord (Gen. 6:9). He obeyed right away when God announced His plans. Noah worked hard building the gigantic, seaworthy Ark and storing up food for hundreds of animals.

"When everything was ready, the Lord said to Noah, "Go into the boat with all your family, for among all the people of the earth, I can see that you alone are righteous."

– Genesis 7:1

So the point I want to make here is that you will inevitably reap some rewards simply because of who you are connected to. In the Bible, this was true of Noah's family. His wife and children didn't do anything special in order to be saved from the flood. They were able to get onto the Ark solely because they were Noah's family. The Bible doesn't state nor does it suggest there was any other reason that they were allowed on the boat and others were not. The blessing that Noah received was automatically funneled to his family simply because they were connected to him.

DON'T BE NAIVE

I know you may be reading this and thinking that you can handle negative personalities when you are confronted with them. You may be thinking that you're pretty strong and you won't be affected by that type of stuff.

But it's virtually impossible to live your life completely unaffected by other people. Their attitudes and opinions are constantly shaping your perspective and influencing your decisions even when you don't realize it. That's why the goal of this chapter is to help you look closely at those connections that don't line up with your destiny, disconnect from them and then seek out godly connections that sharpen you.

"As iron sharpens iron, so a friend sharpens a friend."
- Proverbs 27:17

- *Think about the people you are connected to today. Are the majority of them people you are similar to or are they different from you?*

_____

_____

_____

- *What do you have in common with the people you just thought about? What differences do you have with them that could present a problem in the future?*

_____

_____

_____

I can think of several times in my life when I allowed the negative influence of others to cause me to ignore my better judgment. Many of my missteps are easier for me to see now in hindsight. It can become tempting for me to believe that since I've gotten older, I'm above the influence of other people. But I want to remind you that we all still have a blind spot. Many of these influences are very subtle and you can't afford to let your guard down with this. We are all susceptible to being influenced by ungodly thoughts and attitudes and we have to be on guard at all times.

"Guard your heart above all else, for it determines the course of your life." – Proverbs 4:23

• *Disappointment occurs when our expectations don't match reality. Think about a relationship in which you have experienced disappointment. What things were you expecting to receive from the other person that they could not give you?*

_____

_____

_____

_____

• *Looking at the "potential" in people is not inherently bad but it can become dangerous when we enter into a relationship based solely on the future potential of the other person. The reason being is because we could be setting the other person up to try and give us something they are not capable of giving. In what ways can you step back and change your approach to relationship building and allow someone to prove their abilities before you engage in any sort of exchange with them?*

_____

_____

_____

_____

EVEN THINGS OUT

"Don't team up with those who are unbelievers. How can righteousness be a partner with wickedness? How can light live with darkness?" - 2 Corinthians 6:14

This scripture is where we get the term *unequally yoked*. When you read this text in the Kings James Version of the Bible it explicitly says *"Be not unequally yoked together with an unbeliever"*. Generally when you hear this term of being unequally yoked, it is used to describe dating relationships and marriages with a member of the opposite sex where two people are not equal in their faith. But I want to stress to you that being equally yoked is important in all types of relationships, not just in dating and marriage. In order to fully understand what being unequally yoked looks like, we need to first look at what being equally yoked looks like.

Now I must state that the term "equally yoked" does not actually appear in the Bible. But I do believe that if two people can be "unequally yoked" there must also be an opposite side to that. Again, the text in mention is not referring specifically to marriage so I don't want you to get caught up in the assumption that this portion of the chapter will be all about that. This scripture is speaking about partnerships of all kinds.

In the natural sense of the word, a yoke is a wooden bar that is used to join two oxen to each other in order for them to be able to pull a burden of some sort as a team. Generally this burden was a wagon or a cart used by a farmer to harvest their crops. An equally yoked team of oxen would be of equal strength and stature.

An "unequally yoked" team of oxen would have one stronger ox and one weaker ox, or one taller ox and one shorter ox. As you might expect, the weaker or shorter ox would walk more slowly than the taller, stronger one. This would cause the team of oxen to go around in circles. When oxen were unequally yoked, they couldn't perform the task set before them. Instead of working together, they were working against each other.

In order to have your best year ever, you've got to learn to recognize those places in your life where you're tolerating dysfunction and ask God for the courage to cut it off.

• *Are there areas in your life where you feel like you're going in circles? Maybe you are pulling more weight than your partner or maybe the duties assigned to your team are unbalanced? List whatever comes up for you.*

_____

_____

_____

_____

• *Are there areas in your life where you are not pulling your share of the load? How can you step up and even things back out?*

_____

_____

ARE YOUR RELATIONSHIPS RECIPROCAL?

"Two people are better off than one, for they can help each other succeed. If one person falls, the other can reach out and help. But someone who falls alone is in real trouble. Likewise, two people lying close together can keep each other warm. But how can one be warm alone? A person standing alone can be attacked and defeated, but two can stand back-to-back and conquer. Three are even better, for a triple-braided cord is not easily broken."

- Ecclesiastes 4:9-12

When I read this scripture, the theme that immediately leaped off the page was reciprocation. The scripture says *'they help each other succeed'* and *'keep each other warm'*. One person doesn't benefit more than the other in the type of relationship this scripture is talking about. The relationship in and of itself is actually a vehicle that helps them both succeed. They even fight together and win because they are fighting towards a common goal. They are *equally yoked*.

Ask yourself *"What are you building each of your relationships on?"* Again, I don't want you to get so focused on relationships as only being connections between you and a member of the opposite sex. Relationships extend far beyond that. Every area of your life is relational to some degree. It's critical that your connections are

133

balanced and not one-sided even when you're doing business with someone. It's necessary to have that third cord mentioned in verse 12, which is God, intertwined into every relationship you have.

Are there some relationships in your life that are not reciprocating love and support back to you? I used to struggle with what I now know was a false sense of humility. I used to give, give, give and then turn around and tell myself that I didn't want anything in return because I was serving others. Don't get me wrong. We should serve others. We are commanded by God to do that. But after a while if you keep giving out without getting anything in return you will soon find yourself depleted.

Now it's time to reflect on what you just read and write down your thoughts on the following questions:

• *Go back and read Ecclesiastes 4:9-12 from your own Bible. If possible, read this scripture in at least 3 different Bible translations to expand your understanding of it. Write down the truth of those verses in your own words here:*

_____

_____

_____

_____

• *Look at your closest relationships. How are each of the relationships reciprocating love back to you as described in Ecclesiastes 4:9-12? Are there any obvious areas you have settled in and are you tolerating any behaviors that don't reciprocate love back to you?*

WHAT DO YOU DO WHEN YOU CAN'T CUT PEOPLE OFF?

Earlier in this chapter I stated that there are some relationships that you can't just cut off. Your family members are a perfect example of this. Most of us are not in a position to just walk away from them and in most cases that's not what we want to do or what we feel is right anyway. So what do you do when a family member is literally making your life miserable with their negativity? How should you deal with being obligated as a family member if you're struggling with confusion and betrayal?

One of the first things you have to accept is that just because they're family doesn't mean they will be a safe place for you to lean on or confide in. Not every family tie is built on mutual respect and support. Sometimes "family" simply means that you share the same bloodline.

"Jesus asked, "Who is My mother? Who are My brothers?" Then He pointed to His disciples and said, "Look, these are My mother and brothers. Anyone who does the will of My Father in heaven is My brother and sister and mother!" - Matthew 12:46-50

In order to maintain your own sanity it's important that you realize although you're commanded to love them, they might not be the right person to be spending time with every day, *family or not.* You do not have to neglect yourself, especially your mental health, just because they do. If you have to live with that person, make sure you get as much alone time as you need to rest and recharge.

Even though it may be hard to do, you can't take their behavior personally. It could be that they are going through a difficult time in their own life and may not know how to articulate what they really feel. They may be sick or worried or lacking what they need in terms of love and emotional support. When this is the case it almost always makes it difficult for them to give that same level of love and support to someone else because they lack it themselves. Unfortunately, the people closest to them usually get the backlash of their misplaced emotions.

Either way, ask God for strength to confront what doesn't work in your life. Also, ask God to grant you wisdom to repair those relationships in your life that may need fixing but are yet divinely orchestrated by Him.

• *Find at least 3 Bible scriptures that demonstrate how God wants you to respond to negative people that you encounter and list them here.*

_____

_____

_____

_____

• *In 2 Corinthians 12:6-7 the Apostle Paul says, "Even if I should choose to boast, I would not be a fool, because I would be speaking the truth. But I refrain, so no one will think more of me than is warranted by what I do or say, even though I have received such wonderful revelations from God. So to keep me from becoming proud, I was given a thorn in my flesh, a messenger from Satan to torment me and keep me from becoming proud." Read 2 Corinthians 12 in its entirety and write your insights as to what the Apostle Paul is talking about here.*

_____

_____

_____

_____

* *How can dealing with difficult family members strengthen your character? What can those situations teach you about true humility?*

_____

_____

_____

_____

IT'S SO HARD TO SAY GOOD BYE

I don't want to oversimplify the process of letting go of people and things because it can be tough. Relationships, bad habits and even small tasks like cleaning out your closet and giving away old articles of clothing can become giants of resistance when the time comes to part ways with stuff.

My grandmother had an old trunk in her home. This was the place she would put all the clothes, blankets, toys

137

and other random things that didn't really have a place anywhere else in the house.

Over time, old memories can begin to collect in our heart like those items in my grandmother's trunk. After constantly stuffing things in them day after day, our "mental" trunks can become so full that we don't really even know what's in them anymore! We can't decipher what's usable and what's not.

Each day we fill it with all of the mistakes, heartbreaks and failures we face. Inevitably, that trunk becomes heavier and heavier over time. The increasing weight of it makes it more difficult to carry around. And although it's those moments that have made you who you are today; they can also hold you back from fully becoming the person God truly wants you to be now and in the future.

Memories carry with them an emotional attachment. They remind us of how things used to be. No doubt, some memories can be beautiful and worth holding on to but sadly there are others that serve as painful reminders of our past mistakes and low points. They can keep you stuck in the past. So the key question is how do we know when to *"hold 'em and when to fold 'em?"* Whenever I need help making decisions of the heart, I go directly to God's word.

"The blessing of the Lord makes a person rich, and He adds no sorrow with it." - Proverbs 10:22

The word rich in this scripture isn't only talking about money. The Hebrew meaning of rich also means to 'enrich' one's self. The things that God blesses you with are easily distinguishable because they add value to you.

This can be through healthy relationships, educational opportunities and other chances to give and receive love in a positive way.

If you're at a point where you feel heavyhearted emotionally this may be a strong indicator that it's time to rid yourself of things and connections with people that no longer serve you or add value to your life. Let's start freeing up space by:

- *Getting rid of anger, unforgiveness and discontentment,*
- *Getting rid of unhealthy habits that drain you physically, spiritually and emotionally,*
- *Letting go of old relationships that didn't work out. Keep in mind there is a reason they're an ex!*
- *Letting go of negative self-talk that keeps you from believing in your gifts and abilities*
- *Letting go of past mistakes and failures. Learn the lesson in them first and then let them go!*

Now this next suggestion may take you for a loop but please promise me you will read this with an open mind. Here goes: *Let go of your past successes.* That's right. Let them go. When we succeed at something it's easy to fall into the trap of settling. We never shoot for more and we just plateau off. We don't go after new levels. We spend all of our time reminiscing on our victories rather than planning, preparing and taking steps towards new achievements. Start making room in your heart to pursue greater things.

Knowing when to let go is liberating. I have yet to find another feeling that compares to this. Now, I'm not telling you to forget everything. That's virtually impossible. You can't un-know what you already know. But I am saying that you will have to reassign meaning to some things and people in your life.

Believe it or not, loneliness can even be a blessing to you. It's in those times that God can remove distractions so we can get to know ourselves and Him on a deeper level. Don't let the fear of leaving a dysfunctional place make you ignore the pain that staying in that situation is bringing you.

Here are some thoughts to ponder on as I wrap up this chapter:

- *If you want your relationships to be different and more fulfilling, something has to change. In what areas can you gain more peace by letting go of a draining relationship?*

_____

_____

_____

_____

- *Do you believe it's possible to be unequally yoked with another Christian? Why or why not?*

_____

_____

_____

_____

LESSON #10 – TRUST THE PROCESS

"Frequently remind yourself that God is with you, that He will never fail you, that you can count upon him. Say these words, "God is with me, helping me."
- Norman Vincent Peale

My philosophy on life is that you already have what you need inside of you to do what you've been called to do. But when you put your focus on racing to the finish line trying to obtain the *promise*, it becomes easy to despise the *process*. It's the *process* that stands between us and our desired goal. It's the challenging area of life in between where we are now and where we want to be.

There have been many times that I was so eager to see the "tree" manifest in my life that I didn't recognize that God had already given me everything I needed to have in order to prosper which was a "seed". We must nurture the gifts that God has already put in us in order to see the manifestation of fruit in our life. If God just gave us everything without us having to put skin in the game we would never grow and mature in Christ.

What are you doing with what God has already given you to work with? You can't be jealous of how someone else's tree is budding if you don't fertilize and cultivate what God has entrusted you with. That's what being a good steward is all about. Your success is directly correlated to your work ethic and your faith. It's up to you to nurture that seed in order for it to reach its full potential.

WHAT SIZE SHOE ARE YOU WEARING?

I absolutely love shoes! Shoe shopping is one of my favorite "pastimes" if you will. And if you're like me and you love shoes too I'm sure you know that generally the best looking shoes are not the most comfortable ones to wear. What's funnier is that even shoes that are the right size for your feet can cause you pain until you've worn them long enough to break them in. It may take months before the shoes begin to loosen up and conform to your feet. However, if you never wear the shoes thinking about how much they will hurt your feet, it's unlikely that you will ever break them in and get used to walking in them.

When you're walking in your purpose, it's just as if you are walking in a pair of shoes designed by God that He has made just for you. No one else's feet can fit in them. But here's the catch. Even though these shoes are your correct size, it doesn't mean you won't encounter periods of discomfort as you wear them along the way. And if you let the fear of pain keep you from walking in your purpose, you will find yourself always playing it small and eventually you will be confined to your comfort zone.

Have you ever stepped out into a new endeavor and found yourself thinking, *"Why am I doing this? Is all this hard work even worth it? What was I thinking to feel I could actually do all of this?"* Well if you have, you're not alone. Most normal people have these thoughts all the time. Even those crazy-successful people who make everything they do look super easy have those types of thoughts too.

"For I know the plans I have for you," says the Lord.
"They are plans for good and not for disaster, to give you a
future and a hope." - Jeremiah 29:11

Here God promises that His plans for us would be good. He also lets us know that we won't be hurt in the process. But He never says anywhere in the scripture that He would let us know what the future plans were. So in order for you to have your best year ever, you have to *trust the process.*

"It was by faith that Abraham obeyed when God called him
to leave home and go to another land that God would give
him as his inheritance. He went without knowing where he
was going." – Hebrews 11:8

This is a faith walk. I can teach you all the goal-setting techniques out there but if you don't catch this faith thing none of that will do you any good. In this scripture in Hebrews, it talks about Abraham who is known as the Father of Faith. God made an everlasting covenant with Abraham (See Genesis 17) but in order for that to happen there were some things that Abraham had to do. First, he had to leave everything that was familiar to him and go to a place that God hadn't revealed to him yet. The scripture here lets us know that *"He went without knowing where he was going"*. Even though he had no clue of what was up ahead, Abraham obeyed God and went anyway. The key

143

here is that he took action on what God told him to do and he didn't question it.

- *Read Genesis 15:1-6. What does God promise to do for Abraham? How does Abraham respond to what God shows him? What promises has God made to you that you have found hard to believe?*

_____

_____

_____

_____

Sometimes I feel like we can have more faith in a chair than we do in God. I say that because when was the last time you questioned a chair about its ability to hold you up before you sat down in it? I can't think of one time that I've done that. But I *can* recall times when I have questioned God about things that were going on in my life when I didn't understand or trust what He was doing. We don't question the chair because we have faith that it will do what it was designed to do. We need to have that same level of unwavering faith in the One who created us and the chair.

- *Read Genesis 17. By reading this you see that when God gets ready to elevate you from where you currently are to another level, things about you will have to change. Here God changed their names. When you think of your life and where you are in your own process, what does this chapter say to you? Does change scare you? Why or why not?*

_____

_____

TRANSFORMATION

You may be looking at what your life looks like right now and maybe what you see is not all that great. But don't mistake Gods delay for your final destiny. In nature, the caterpillar shows no indication that it will ever be a beautiful butterfly. If we simply look at the caterpillar for where it is now, we will miss out on its amazing destiny.

Imagine this: *What if the caterpillar told God that she didn't want to change? What if she complained to God about how tight it was going to be inside the cocoon? I mean, what if she never came out of that thing? Being a caterpillar might not be all that glamorous but at least she'd know what to expect if she stayed like she was!*

I've found myself having conversations with God like this. I started to shrink back when the process got hard. I would have rather stayed small and close to the familiar because launching out into the unknown was too scary.

Wouldn't it be awesome if we could just go to our next level without having to go through a season of darkness? But when you truly go to the next level it will always require a new you. And you can't become that new you without going through a "cocoon type process" to manifest the new you. The cocoon is scary because the form that you used to have is no more. And who you shall be hasn't manifested either. The process of becoming a new creation means you will have to go thru a season of nothingness.

"Oh Lord, You are our Father and we are the clay and You are our potter. We are all the work of Your hands."

- Isaiah 64:8

I love this scripture because it reminds me of how special we are in Gods eyes. God Himself molded and shaped us with His own hands. Isaiah talks about us being clay in this passage. Before clay has been molded by a skilled potter it starts out as a shapeless blob. It's not until it goes through a process where it has to be molded and allowed to harden, that it can become a useable vessel.

As the potter molds and shapes the clay on the wheel, he will inevitably discover defects in the clay. He has the power to either allow the defects to stay or he can reshape the pottery to get rid of them. Just like an earthly potter, God has power to reshape us. It is not His desire that we have defects in us so He will continue to work and re-work us to make us into useful vessels. But if we resist Gods molding and shaping, we will eventually harden the wrong way. We should not resist God's reshaping of our lives if we want to be used for Kingdom work.

In the process of creating pottery, once a potter has molded the clay into the shape they desire it has to then go through the drying process. This is where the vessel dries to a leather-like condition before it goes through the final step which is the firing process. Pottery must be fired at a temperature high enough to mature the clay, meaning that the high temperature hardens the vessel to enable it to hold water which is the very thing it was designed to do. If it doesn't go through that last stage it won't be able to be used for its purpose.

"Dear friends, we are already Gods children but He has not yet shown us what we shall be like when Christ appears. But we do know that we will be like Him, for we will see Him as He is." - 1 John 3:2

We all have to go through a metamorphosis process in order for God to transform us. You might be in a place that is so low and so dry right now that you aren't sure if you can pull through it this time. But when you stop trying to figure out *why* you are going through the process and just start embracing the process, you will see that the place that seemed like it would be your *tomb* was really your *cocoon*. You will learn that the place you thought you would die in was really just your place of preparation for greatness!

"Now all glory to God, who is able, through His mighty power at work within us, to accomplish infinitely more than we might ask or think." - Ephesians 3:20

- *Why is persistent prayer so important when we are going through the "cocoon" process?*

_____

_____

_____

_____

LESSON #11 – BEATING BURN OUT

"Never overestimate the strength of the torchbearer's arm,
for even the strongest arms grow weary."

— A.J. Darkholme

As women, there will come a time in each of our lives that we will run out of steam because of all the constant demands that are placed on us. We can give of ourselves so much to the point where we become physically, mentally and spiritually depleted. Before we know it, the burning flame of enthusiasm that we had for our work, our family and God is extinguished by exhaustion and fatigue.

How can you get back to a state of vigor for life after you've hit the brick wall of burn out? Here are some tips that helped me to get back in the swing of things when I found myself tapped out. Please remember that these are not magical, overnight solutions. Just like you gradually got to the point of burn out, you must take gradual and intentional steps to get back in the game.

First, you must eliminate energy drainers and learn how to say no. This can be tough because many of the things that can drain us the most are usually connections that are beyond our control like family or things that are related to our livelihood such as our job. If this is the case, you may have to set some firm boundaries regarding your time with family members as well as restate your expectations of them. Also you need to be very clear about what they can reasonably expect from you moving forward. Remember: cut out activities you find yourself doing "just because". You have to realize that you cannot be all things for all people. At some point, you have to put your needs ahead of others. And that should not be taken in a selfish context. Society tends to lean towards the idea that we should push ourselves to our limit and even in the church we can "serve" until the point of burn out if we aren't careful. It can also be easy to feel guilty when we want to scale back and check in with our self. But here's why you shouldn't feel guilty:

When you take a plane ride and the flight attendant goes over the emergency procedures with the passengers, in the event the plane has a loss of cabin pressure they instruct you to place the mask over your own face first before you help other people. You have to make sure that you are okay or you won't be around very long to help anyone else even if you wanted to. Saying no is tough because we don't want to offend people or let anyone down. But if you work to develop consistency in doing this, over time people will learn to respect your decisions and your reasons for saying no.

In order for you to accomplish what God has for you to do, you have to take care of yourself and you can't spread yourself too thin. The Bible tells us that God wants us to prosper in our health in the same way we prosper spiritually.

So we have to take care of ourselves naturally so. Make sure you are drinking enough water, eating the right foods and getting some exercise each day. It has to become a lifestyle. Doing these things every now and then won't help you get out of your slump. I recommend making just a few changes at a time so that you don't go back into overwhelm and quit. Make the first step that you are comfortable with changing and stick with it before you move to another one if consistency is a challenge for you.

If you are struggling with constantly feeling overwhelmed, make sure your priorities are in line with the will of God for your life. The truth is there are some things that we have made a priority in our lives that are not a priority with God. They may even be good things but they may not be in line with our purpose.

We must keep "first things first". Ask yourself these questions if you are having trouble figuring out what needs to go:

- *Does this activity really have to be done now or even done at all?*

- *Is what I am doing necessary for my livelihood or the well-being and safety of myself and my family?*

- *Look at all the obligations you have on your plate right now. Of those things, which ones can wait until another time or be eliminated all together? List them here.*

_____

_____

_____

_____

There are simply some things that we work around the clock for with hopes for certain gains but the things that we are doing are outside of the true will of God for our lives. It's important that you look at those things and phase out of them or stop doing them all together as soon as you can to cut down on overwhelm.

Another thing you can do to start seeing the light of day is to de-clutter your physical environment. This may be one the easiest areas to rectify in a short amount of time if you solicit help. Your physical environment is generally a reflection of your mental state. More often than not, if your home and work space is unorganized and cluttered, so are your thoughts. I chose to hire a professional organizer to help speed up the efficiency of this task.

Moreover, if you have reached a place where you feel like you are drowning under all your responsibilities, *ask for help*. I think one of the things that stop us from doing this is that asking for help can be perceived as a sign of weakness. This is untrue. As women we are naturally equipped to juggle a lot of tasks but often we do so at a rate that is unsustainable. Asking for help is actually a sign of true wisdom.

"Moses continued, "At that time I told you, 'You are too great a burden for me to carry all by myself. The Lord your God has increased your population, making you as numerous as the stars! And may the Lord, the God of your ancestors, multiply you a thousand times more and bless you as he promised! But you are such a heavy load to carry! How can I deal with all your problems and bickering? Choose some well-respected men from each tribe who are known for their wisdom and understanding, and I will appoint them as your leaders.' "Then you responded, 'Your plan is a good one.'"

- Deuteronomy 1:9-18

Look at what Moses had to do here in this example from the Bible. He was drowning under all of the demands of leading the nation of Israel. He had to put people in place to help share the load. If you feel like you are overwhelmed or experiencing depression, it's wise to talk with someone about how you are feeling by seeking professional help. This could include a variety of individuals such as a counselor, your pastor, a spiritual mentor or a trusted friend. A skilled professional can help you restructure your mental processes by talking things out. They can help you learn to recognize when you are burning the candle at both ends and help you prevent future bouts of burn out.

Reconnecting with God may be the most critical of all the things that you do to help rejuvenate your desire for life and work. Imagine for a moment that a plug to an appliance becomes disconnected from its power socket. No matter how many different ways you push the on switch to that appliance; it will not come on until it is connected to a source of power. The same goes with us as women. There are times when the busyness of life's affairs will cause us to become disconnected from our supernatural power source which is God. We must reconnect ourselves to Him through sincere prayer as well as get enough rest to allow our bodies to recharge.

You will indefinitely have to physically separate from distractions and quiet yourself through prayer and meditation to clearly hear from Him. Rest for your physical body is necessary for many reasons. First, you are better able to focus when you are rested and it improves your mood. We are less likely to get sick when we are well rested also. Take a simple lesson from our Creator. Even He rested after creating the universe so you should too.

After working through all of the above steps in my own struggle with burn out, I must admit that there still came a day when I had to look at myself in the mirror, think about the mission ahead of me and push! I had to push through what I felt like and realize that every day I will not always feel like going forward but I still have to because people are counting on me to be in place. I had to remind myself that God's plan is bigger than the temporary feeling that I was experiencing at the moment.

- *Have you ever found yourself at a place where you were burned out? What factors do you think contributed to your struggles with burn out? (Pushing yourself too hard, challenging life circumstances, not caring for yourself physically, etc.)*

- *What did the symptoms of burn out look like for you? What was your wakeup call to let you know you needed to make a change?*

Grab your Bible and go to the book of Psalm. Something that I found to be fascinating was that the Psalmists often used, especially in their songs of frustration and desperation, the words "I will" when it came to getting out of their slump. This means no matter how you feel you have to be determined to put yourself in a place where God can reinfuse life back into you. That means you must engage in personal times of prayer, worship services with other believers, meditation and even just sitting in God's presence. Look at the areas you are being fought the most in and instead of "trying", be determined and create "I will" statements. Here are some of mine:

- *"I will get out of bed and start my day in prayer."*

- *"I will recite my affirmations after prayer" so I can remind myself of what God thinks about me.*

- *"I will drink 3 liters of water today" so that I can keep my body properly hydrated.*

- *"I will keep a thankful heart throughout the day" to let God know I appreciate Him.*

- *"I will ignore negative thoughts and comments" that cause me to doubt what God has said in His word.*

- *Take some time to create your own "I will" statements and jot them down here.*

_____

_____

_____

_____

_____

_____

_____

_____

_____

LESSON #12 – HEAL FROM YOUR PAST

"Sometimes it's the scars that remind you that you survived. Sometimes the scars tell you that you have healed."
— *Ashley D. Wallis*

We all have a past. I don't care how you try to twist it or run from it. It's an inevitable truth. Our past can hold us hostage with memories and experiences that are so painful it causes us to panic at the thought of taking a step forward. But if you allow your past to dictate your life, you will never see how far you've truly come when you stay focused on what's behind you. God took into consideration all of your flaws when He called you. And despite areas where you may have missed the mark, you still have a chance to right the wrongs of your past. God's grace and forgiveness gives us another shot at happiness.

"For everyone has sinned; we all fall short of God's glorious standard." - Romans 3:23

Back when I was in junior high school, I used to play basketball. I wasn't half bad either for a vertically challenged thirteen year old with two left feet! I'm sure you

159

know that in the game of basketball, there's a thing called a foul. Webster's Dictionary defines a foul as an act in a sport involving physical contact with deliberate roughing up of an opponent. On the occasion that I actually played in a game it was enough for me to just get the ball down the court; so when I got fouled it really got under my skin!

But the redeeming fact of getting fouled was that even though that interference caused me to miss the initial shot, it gave me an opportunity to shoot a *free throw* or as I often called it – my second chance to save face in front of the people in the stands! There were times when my coach would make us devote our entire practice time to shooting free throws. Our coach worked us hard in this area. He told us there were going to be games in which a free throw would be the deciding factor between a win and a loss. We needed to get the technique of shooting free throws down to a science.

In one of the final games of the season, I remember standing at the free throw line in that game after I'd just been fouled. I bounced the ball for a few seconds, raised it up, positioned it, released it and followed through. *Boing!* My heart sank.

The ball bounced off the rim causing me to miss the shot. Nevertheless, I still had a second free throw and this time I refocused my energy and replayed what I was taught in all those practices. I remembered the visualization techniques my coach taught me. I remembered how he taught me to steady my hand and block out the noise of the crowd. And in that moment, I raised the ball, released it and followed through. This time the ball went in. *I made the shot!*

"What shall we say about such wonderful things as these? If God is for us, who can ever be against us? Since He did not spare even His own Son but gave Him up for us all, won't He also give us everything else? Who dares accuse us whom God has chosen for His own? No one—for God Himself has given us right standing with Himself. Who then will condemn us? No one—for Christ Jesus died for us and was raised to life for us, and He is sitting in the place of honor at God's right hand, pleading for us. Can anything ever separate us from Christ's love? Does it mean He no longer loves us if we have trouble or calamity, or are persecuted, or hungry, or destitute, or in danger, or threatened with death? (As the Scriptures say, "For your sake we are killed every day; we are being slaughtered like sheep.") No, despite all these things, overwhelming victory is ours through Christ, who loved us." - *Romans 8:31-37*

This scripture shows us there is a bright side to our dark past. Life will send fouls your way and the enemy will always try to tell you that you've done too much for God to use you. But Christ died and rose again so that the things that used to serve shame in your life can now serve a purpose. You can help someone because you now know how to overcome in that area. So learn from your past and forgive yourself. Your past doesn't define you; it only prepares you for your greater calling.

- *Does the pain of your hurt seem so great and personal that you find it difficult to share with other people? What is holding you back from sharing at times?*

_____

_____

_____

_____

- *Perhaps you have opened up to share your hurts before, and people did not react like you expected. Do you ever feel like no one understands or can relate to your pain?*

_____

_____

_____

_____

GET SERIOUS

When I became intentional about my personal and spiritual development, the first thing I did was take inventory of my life. By doing this I realized that for a long time I was looking to external things for happiness. I found myself blaming those external circumstances for where I was or wasn't in life. And while some of those outside factors did play a part in where I was, I had to own up to the fact that my positioning in life was the sum total of my own decisions.

Even though I couldn't pinpoint the exact time in my life in which I was derailed so to speak, at some point I'd chosen a path that led me to a place of emotional and spiritual bankruptcy. I'm sure most people on the outside looking in at my life believed I had it all together but I knew the truth. On the inside I was missing something that no one could see with a natural eye. Internally I was deteriorating. It was a gradual decline. It took time for me to get there so it would take even more time for me to get out of it.

I was only able to get to higher ground by first surrendering and telling myself that what I was doing wasn't working. I had to face the reality that, yes, there were things outside of my control that contributed to my situation but the biggest driving factor of where I was in my life emotionally, physically and spiritually was because of my choices. And when I came to myself and finally declared that the path I was on was a destructive one, only then was I able to open my heart up to the power of God's grace. It felt good to know that no matter how far I'd gone down the wrong road, it wasn't too late to turn around.

But in order to make the complete turnaround I had to look at myself in the mirror and ask:

• *Did I choose to pursue something that I got a clear signal from God to leave alone and now I'm hurt as a result?*

• *Did I choose to compromise when I should have held up my standard?*

• *Did I choose to carry the burden of anger when I had the option to forgive the offense and be free?*

By turning the mirror back on me I realized that much of what I had experienced was self-inflicted wounds. We are all blessed with the ability to choose. That's the great part about it. We often take ourselves through more than we have to because we choose to hold on to something God is telling us to release.

I remember the day very vividly in which I made the vow that I would no longer toil over things and people I couldn't control. I released the anxiety around "the thought" of what could have happened. When you conjure up scenarios and replay them in your mind all day, at that point, all you're doing is managing the *what if's* of something. But you're far from dealing with the actual reality of it.

- *What would my life have been like if my dad had raised me?*
- *What would my life have been like if my marriage would have worked?*
- *What would my life be like if they would have stayed?*

I'm sure you can come up with some other statements like these to add to this list based on your own experiences. Each of the statements I listed are things you will never know for sure. And who's to say if you stayed connected with some of the stuff you desire to hold on to that things would have turned out better? It's just as likely that they could have turned out worse. This is the point where you have to fully trust God that you're exactly where He wants you to be. You have to know that all things are working together in your best interest. Look at rejection from people as divine redirection from God! He won't use any person or thing that left you to bless you.

- *How has hurt changed you from who you were before those hurtful events occurred to who you are now?*

_____

_____

_____

_____

- *If you feel like you have changed for the worse, read Psalm 119:71. Read it in at least 3 different translations if possible. According to this scripture, what is the blessing that comes through times of suffering even if it's at the hands of people we love?*

_____

_____

_____

_____

LET GO OF OFFENSE FROM OTHERS

There were many instances in my life where I felt like holding an offense against the person who hurt me was hurting them. Not forgiving the other person doesn't stop God from carrying out His plan for their future but it can stop Him from carrying out His plan for yours. Maybe the following illustration can help explain it better.

If I hold a big rock over my head for 30 seconds it will still weigh the same amount as when I sit it back down on the ground. If I choose to take that same rock and hold it over my head for an hour, by the end of that hour chances are I'll be experiencing great pain. Here's the truth: Just like holding on to the rock didn't change how heavy it was, neither will holding on to an offense. Choosing to hold the rock over my head instead of putting it down caused me to endure unnecessary pain and it still didn't change the weight of the rock.

Let that sink in. When you really grasp what I'm saying down in your soul, you can begin the process of healing and forgiving in a real way. Resenting someone doesn't change what they did. And when you adopt the mindset that holding on to what was done is going to somehow erase or lessen the hurt, it's just like holding a rock over your head. It becomes pointless and you'll endure self-inflicted pain.

When you make a mistake, it's important that you learn the lesson you were meant to learn so that you don't begin a destructive cycle. And once that lesson is realized it's even more important that you learn to have compassion on yourself and move forward.

- *Has your reaction to hurt or offense in your life ever resulted in you trying to get revenge on the person that hurt you? If so, explain why you felt that getting revenge or wounding the person who offended you would resolve your problem. Would that resolution bring lasting peace, or only add to your pain as a victim?*

_____

_____

_____

_____

IT'S ALL ABOUT HOW YOU LOOK AT IT

Your healing starts with you and the way you think. It begins with you choosing to adopt the right perspective regarding the things that have happened in your life. You actually have to give a situation power over you to influence how you think, what you think and even the frequency that you think it. It all starts and ends in your head. Don't give your past pain power over you. It's bad enough that it affected you in your past. Don't let it have your future.

What you think sets the tone for how you will love (or not love) others. It lays the foundation for the way you love yourself. You can't start to forgive others or yourself until you realize how important the act of forgiveness is in your process of healing. I know that there will be times in life in which pain is inevitable but there are also times when you can introduce pain into your own life by contending with God for things that aren't in His divine design for your life. Ignoring red flags won't make them go away. God will never let you be deceived. But when you ignore clear warnings from God whether He sends the warning through another person or by other means, you are in essence deceiving yourself.

I get some pretty severe migraine headaches from time to time. The pain can get so bad that it can stop me dead in my tracks. Like these migraines, more times than not we would probably ignore some issues in our life and fail to seek help if it were not for the signals that make us stop and take notice.

Have you ever had your heart broken before? After a bad break up I had, I became tempted to let bitterness seep in. I even began to question God about why He would allow me to go through an experience like that if He loved me. God showed me that I was seeking to fill a deeper void. I had to go through it because answers will often emerge from our experiences. We may never fully understand the lesson until we go through it.

God loves you so much and He will allow you to experience disappointment to signal to you that something is wrong below the surface of your heart. Maybe you've lost your focus? It could be that you aren't praying or spending as much time with God as you should be? Idols can quickly materialize in our life without warning.

- *What characteristics in your life might indicate that you haven't fully forgiven and let go of past hurts, even if you know in your heart it's what you need to do?*

_____

_____

_____

_____

WHAT'S THE PURPOSE OF FORGIVENESS?

If we are going to live the beautiful, abundant lives that God intended for us to live from the very beginning, forgiveness has to become a daily practice. If you spend your days holding on to bitterness, hurt and resentment; you won't have space in your heart to allow good things to come in. More importantly, unforgiveness stands between you and God. We are all sinners. And it's through grace that God has forgiven us and sees us as righteous.

"For God made Christ, who never sinned, to be the offering for our sin, so that we could be made right with God through Christ." - 2 Corinthians 5:21

When I think about what had to be given up in order for me to have access to eternal life, I can find a way to forgive others even if it's hard for me to do. I'm not saying that I'll partner with someone who has wronged me or even continue to fellowship with that person but I will forgive them and release myself from any future bondage around that situation. I do believe that there are some situations where cutting ties is the best thing to do. It's ok to burn some bridges especially if they should have never been crossed in the first place!

Forgiveness is first for your benefit, not for the benefit of the person you are forgiving. As long as you are playing the role of a victim, you are carrying a heavy burden. Forgiveness allows you to lay down the pain and walk away from it free from the bondage it carries with it. When you choose to be unforgiving, you become stuck in a bad rerun of your past.

If you have been hurt by someone, especially a significant other or a family member, you have to choose to let what they did go if you're going to remain in the relationship. If not, you are opening up the door for the spirit of offense to take root in your heart. You will inevitably push the relationship to a place in which it will become unsalvageable. Besides, it's unfair for you to choose to stay in the relationship and then continue to spend your time reminding them of their mistake, criticizing them and never allowing them a chance to live the situation down.

THE ESSENCE OF FORGIVENESS

The process of forgiving someone is a very special one in which you literally must completely let go of any ill feelings towards another person, towards yourself, or towards a situation. And I'll take it a step further. Forgiveness is like releasing the debt someone owes you and not expecting exact punishment for the offense they committed.

This is not always easy to do. In fact, it is very difficult but you cannot let that stop you from trying. Because the truth is that you can't do this in your own strength anyway. You have to call on God to help you do what you need to do for your own healing. It's going to take more than lip service to do this. It's more than just saying "I forgive you". It's a mental process. You'll have to empty your mind of hateful, vengeful and angry thoughts and this won't happen spontaneously or quickly. That's why I'm stressing that it's a process.

You can't just forgive one time and then that's it. You will have to develop daily habits and practices that shift your way of thinking. For me, I constantly remind myself of the grace that I'm extended and that I'm now charged with giving that same grace to others without expecting something in return.

Forgiveness allows you to take responsibility for your own happiness. You will always be frustrated if your happiness relies on someone else to do the right thing in order for you to gain peace. That's too much power to give another person. Take your power back!

When you choose to learn from pain, what you went through will make you wiser - *not bitter*. Once you truly learn the lesson behind why a negative relationship entered into your life, you will no longer attract situations and future relationships that attempt to teach you the same lesson. You will graduate and inevitably grow and as a result you won't keep repeating the same unpleasant cycle over and over again.

GIVE PEOPLE THE BENEFIT OF THE DOUBT

There's an old saying that says "Hurt people – hurt people!" A sure indication that a person is hurt on the inside is shown by what they do on the outside. Showing love in spite of how you're treated can diffuse a bad situation and help healing begin for you and for the other person. Love people for where they are and give them the benefit of the doubt.

The truth is most people really are doing the best they can with what they know to do. And get this: The real you won't be revealed when you are in control of a matter. The real you is shown when you are thrust into situations that are beyond your control. You can't control other people's actions but you can control your reaction to what they do and say. And a lot of times, people you think are "just being mean" are really people who have been deeply hurt and they act that way as a defense mechanism to avoid being hurt again. Believe it or not, you have the power through your reaction to bring healing to someone. They don't need someone to get in the boxing ring with them.

They need unconditional love. Look beyond what they are doing on the outside and look for the deeper root of the issue. Most people aren't mean just to be mean. There's generally something else there causing the behavior.

It will take a lot of God's presence and a lot of prayer to be able to look beyond peoples actions, especially when they are hurtful ones. This means you must live with a prayerful mindset and attitude. It's ok to ask God to help you not be offended each day. Ask Him to keep you in control of your emotions.

The choice is yours. It always has been and it always will be. You have the choice to overcome evil with good and find a new level of joy you didn't know was possible by letting go of offense and choosing to forgive. Allow yourself to heal.

- *How might holding on to unforgiveness, whether that's against others or even against yourself affect your prayers?*

_____

_____

_____

_____

- *How will unforgiveness open the door for the enemy to negatively affect our lives? Describe any evidence of ways that Satan may have gained a foothold in your life because of issues of unforgiveness.*

_____

_____

_____

_____

    • *List 3 scriptures that you can reference to help you reverse those negative effects in your life. Write them here.*

_____

_____

_____

_____

A PRAYER FOR YOUR BEST YEAR EVER!

Recite this prayer to yourself in your quiet time

Dear Heavenly Father:

I am Your child and I come to You as humble as I know how, first thanking You for the Gift You gave me through Your Son Jesus. I thank You for forgiveness of my sins.

Give me a renewed strength and purpose in you God through the Holy Spirit. Keep my tongue from harsh words, my mind from unclean thoughts, my feet from running with the wrong crowd and my heart full of compassion for my fellow brothers and sisters. Remove any selfish ways and agendas that I have that would hinder me from doing your will fully and wholeheartedly.

Give me the courage to trust in You to meet my needs rather than going about things my own way. I will no longer put together my own plan and ask You to bless it. *I will simply ask You for the plan.*

I lay aside every weight in order to thank You for my new year that You are manifesting before my very eyes. I release anything and everything that I have held onto in the past that has weighed me down.

God, I thank You for my new year! I decree and declare that I will not waste this year. 2 Corinthians 5:7 says that if anyone be in You, he is now a new creature. Old things are gone and I am now walking into a new season of consecutive wins! I command old patterns of thought and old ways of living to flee in Jesus name. I declare that new ideas, news ways of being, new opportunities and new purpose over take my life. Detrimental cycles are broken. I declare freedom in You God!

In Jesus Name – Amen!

DAILY JOURNALING PROMPTS

Use these prompts to help spark ideas for you to write about during your prayer and journaling time.

General Journaling Prompts

1. What did you do today?
2. What new lesson did you learn today?
3. In what ways has your perspective changed about certain situations that are happening in your life right now? What caused the change in perspective?
4. How are you feeling right now?
5. What did you read today? What did you discover about yourself as you read?
6. What are your plans for today?
7. Did you complete everything you had planned for yesterday? If NO, what stopped you from finishing them?
8. What's the one thing you must get done today and why?
9. What are you thankful for right now?
10. What made you smile today?
11. What do you love about your life right now?
12. What do you wish you could change about your life right now?
13. What is one thing you wish others knew about you that is often misunderstood by others?
14. What does "enough" look like in your life?

15. When do you feel most energized?

16. Make a list of the people in your life who genuinely support and love you, and who you can genuinely trust. Schedule some time to give them a call "just because" or make time to spend time with them.

17. Write about a time when you got lost in what you were doing or when work didn't feel like work. What activity were you doing?

18. Make a list of everything you'd like to say no to no matter how far you'd have to stretch yourself to find the courage to do so.

19. Make a list of everything you'd like to say yes to no matter how far you'd have to stretch yourself to find the courage to do so.

20. What is stopping you from fully being yourself?

21. Hold a hand mirror in front of your face so that you only see your eyes. Look deeply into your eyes and describe the person in the mirror?

22. Describe the ideal you. How have you already become this person? What aspects of this person are you lacking? What can you do to close that gap of what you are lacking to become your ideal self?

23. What is your favorite childhood memory and why?

24. Describe something you wish everybody had.

Goal Setting Journal Prompts

1. Think of one goal you have right now. Why do you want to accomplish this goal? What will you get out of reaching this goal?
2. What does this goal mean to you? Why is it important to you that you achieve this?
3. Who will be impacted when you achieve this goal?
4. How will this make you feel? What emotions will you have when you accomplish your goal? What are your core desired feelings?
5. What did you do today that moved you closer to reaching your goals?
6. Is there anything you did this week that you wish you'd done differently?
7. Describe a goal you keep putting off and why?
8. Write out your bucket list.
9. Describe a goal that is seemingly out of your reach. Develop a strategy to reach that goal.
10. Dear Past Me …
11. Dear Future Me …
12. Where are you vulnerable?
13. What are your main daily motives?
14. What are your biggest time wasters?
16. What major block in your life needs to be resolved?
17. Where do you need to clarify your stand, position or values?
18. For what problems do you need to ask for solutions?

Relationship Journaling Prompts

1. What is your view on soul mates?
2. How can you start forgiving others who have caused you pain?
3. Finish the following sentence: In the eyes of my ideal mate, I am …
4. What does it mean to love yourself and to accept yourself as you are?
5. How does loving and accepting yourself affect your ability to love and accept others?
6. List the qualities of good communication. Which of these is most important to you and why?
7. What is the most important thing you can do to nurture a loving relationship?
8. List five people, dead or alive, whom you admire. For each person, write a short statement about why you admire each person.
9. At what age did you become aware of your own abilities to make ethical and moral decisions and to choose how you react to others? What happened to bring about this awareness?
10. How do you define a relationship?
11. How was love expressed in your home when you were a child?
12. What models did you have for loving relationships when you were growing up?
13. If someone disagrees with you, how do you deal with it?

14. When things don't go the way you want, how do you handle disappointment?
15. How do you deal with change?
16. For where you are in life right now do you feel you *want* a relationship or do you feel you *need* a relationship? Discuss your response as to why you chose it.
17. Do you find it hard to maintain close, trusting relationships? Why or why not?
18. What does being a friend mean to you?
19. Describe LOVE using all five of your senses.
20. I should forgive or accept ...

ADDITIONAL JOURNALING PAGES

My Best Year Ever!

My Best Year Ever!

My Best Year Ever!

My Best Year Ever!

My Best Year Ever!

_____
_____
_____
_____
_____
_____
_____
_____
_____
_____
_____
_____
_____
_____
_____
_____
_____
_____
_____
_____
_____
_____
_____
_____
_____
_____
_____
_____
_____

My Best Year Ever!

My Best Year Ever!

My Best Year Ever!

My Best Year Ever!

My Best Year Ever!

My Best Year Ever!

My Best Year Ever!

My Best Year Ever!

My Best Year Ever!

_____

_____

_____

_____

_____

_____

_____

_____

_____

_____

_____

_____

_____

_____

_____

_____

_____

_____

_____

_____

_____

_____

_____

_____

_____

_____

_____

_____

_____

_____

My Best Year Ever!

My Best Year Ever!

My Best Year Ever!

My Best Year Ever!

_____
_____
_____
_____
_____
_____
_____
_____
_____
_____
_____
_____
_____
_____
_____
_____
_____
_____
_____
_____
_____
_____
_____
_____
_____
_____
_____
_____
_____
_____

My Best Year Ever!

My Best Year Ever!

_____
_____
_____
_____
_____
_____
_____
_____
_____
_____
_____
_____
_____
_____
_____
_____
_____
_____
_____
_____
_____
_____
_____
_____
_____
_____
_____

My Best Year Ever!

My Best Year Ever!

My Best Year Ever!

_____

_____

_____

_____

_____

_____

_____

_____

_____

_____

_____

_____

_____

_____

_____

_____

_____

_____

_____

_____

_____

_____

_____

_____

_____

_____

_____

My Best Year Ever!

My Best Year Ever!

My Best Year Ever!

My Best Year Ever!

My Best Year Ever!

My Best Year Ever!

My Best Year Ever!

My Best Year Ever!

My Best Year Ever!

My Best Year Ever!

_____

_____

_____

_____

_____

_____

_____

_____

_____

_____

_____

_____

_____

_____

_____

_____

_____

_____

_____

_____

_____

_____

_____

_____

_____

_____

_____

My Best Year Ever!

My Best Year Ever!

My Best Year Ever!

_____

_____

_____

_____

_____

_____

_____

_____

_____

_____

_____

_____

_____

_____

_____

_____

_____

_____

_____

_____

_____

_____

_____

_____

_____

_____

_____

My Best Year Ever!

My Best Year Ever!

My Best Year Ever!

My Best Year Ever!

My Best Year Ever!

_____

_____

_____

_____

_____

_____

_____

_____

_____

_____

_____

_____

_____

_____

_____

_____

_____

_____

_____

_____

_____

_____

_____

_____

_____

_____

My Best Year Ever!

My Best Year Ever!

My Best Year Ever!

My Best Year Ever!

My Best Year Ever!

My Best Year Ever!

My Best Year Ever!

My Best Year Ever!

My Best Year Ever!

My Best Year Ever!

My Best Year Ever!

_____
_____
_____
_____
_____
_____
_____
_____
_____
_____
_____
_____
_____
_____
_____
_____
_____
_____
_____
_____
_____
_____
_____
_____
_____
_____
_____
_____
_____

My Best Year Ever!

ABOUT THE AUTHOR

Rachel L. Proctor is a renowned motivational speaker, author and minister. She is also a well-respected public servant in her hometown of DeSoto, TX. Rachel is the founder of eMErge™ Motivational Coaching which has allowed her to successfully coach hundreds of clients through her online teachings, live events, one on one strategy sessions and daily motivational text messages. And when she's not coaching, you can find her indulging in (and highlighting) the latest John Maxwell book, watching anything on Food Network or shopping for fabulous shoes.

Learn more about Rachel and connect with her over on her inspirational blog at www.RachelLProctor.com.

30673896R00152

Made in the USA
Middletown, DE
02 April 2016